THE MAKING OF MODERN JAPAN

CIVILIZATION AND SOCIETY

Studies in Social, Economic, and Cultural History

General Editor

Theodore K. Rabb, Princeton University

Consulting Editors

Thomas W. Africa, State University of New York, Binghamton
David J. Herlihy, Harvard University
David S. Landes, Harvard University
Henry Rosovsky, Harvard University
Stanley J. Stein, Princeton University
Stephan A. Thernstrom, Harvard University

THE MAKING OF
MODERN JAPAN

KENNETH B. PYLE

University of Washington

D. C. HEATH AND COMPANY
Lexington, Massachusetts • Toronto

International Standard Book Number: 0-669-84657-0

Library of Congress Catalog Card Number: 77-081543

To our parents

ACKNOWLEDGMENTS

I would like to express appreciation to the *Journal of Asian Studies* for permission to include material originally presented in my article "The Technology of Japanese Nationalism," Vol. XXXIII, No. 1 (November 1973), pp. 51–65; to Stanford University Press for permission to include material originally presented in my book *The New Generation in Meiji Japan: Problems of Cultural Identity, 1885–1895* (Stanford, 1969); to the *Journal of Japanese Studies* for permission to include material originally presented in my articles "Advantages of Followership: German Economics and Japanese Bureaucrats, 1890–1925," Vol. I, No. 1 (Autumn 1974), pp. 127–164, "Japan Faces Her Future," Vol. I, No. 2 (Spring 1975), pp. 347–350, and "State and Society in the Interwar Years," Vol. III, No. 2 (Summer 1977), pp. 421–430.

October 1977   Kenneth B. Pyle

PREFACE

My purpose in writing this book is to set forth in rather stark, straightforward fashion some of the main themes in the historical development of modern Japanese society. It is my hope that these themes, culled from a decade of teaching the subject, may prove of value to the person wishing a broad understanding of the emergence of Japan as a world power in modern times. I have tried, in the course of writing, to avoid overwhelming the reader with the names and details that are characteristic of the "past politics" approach to history, and instead to concentrate on the dynamics of historical change.

The rapidity with which Japan industrialized in the late nineteenth century and the unique form that its industrial society took in the twentieth century have attracted wide attention, and that attention intensified as Japan recovered from the devastation of World War Two to become the world's third greatest economic power. Why did the breakthrough to a modern industrial system occur so early in Japan, as compared with other non-Western societies? Much of the American research on Japan in the last twenty-five years has been concerned with understanding how industrialization was initiated. That will be one of the issues we pursue in this book.

How far back in history is it sensible to go in order to describe the emergence of modern Japan? Many historians have begun the story in the middle of the nineteenth century with Commodore Perry's opening of Japan to the Western world. The difficulty with such a starting point is that it leaves the reader with an inadequate understanding of many of the forces that made modern Japan. It tends, in particular, to exaggerate the impact of the West, while overlooking those long-term trends in Japanese society and economy, already at work before the redoubtable Yankee arrived, that created conditions favorable to industrialization.

By their nature historians are prone to move ever further back in time to determine the roots of historical movements. "The explanation of the very recent in terms of the remotest past," wrote Marc Bloch, "naturally attractive to men who have made of this past their chief subject of research, has sometimes dominated our studies to the point of a hypnosis. In its most characteristic aspect, this idol of the historian tribe may be called the obsession with origins."[1] Without wishing to fall under the sway of that idol, I have nonetheless chosen to begin this book with a consideration of the far-reaching reshaping of Japanese institutions that occurred at the end of the sixteenth cen-

[1] Marc Bloch, *The Historian's Craft*, trans. Peter Putnam (New York, 1964), p. 29.

tury. Here we may clearly find the roots of modern Japanese development, for the institutions established at that time set in motion the long-run social and economic trends favorable to industrialization. We therefore begin our account with the unification of Japan at the end of the sixteenth century and the establishment, in the decades that followed, of a novel system of territorial control known as the Tokugawa Bakufu. During the subsequent period 1600–1868, while Japan was governed by the Tokugawa system, the warfare and turbulence of previous centuries disappeared, cities grew, agriculture productivity rose, the country was knit together by improved communications, trade prospered, and population stabilized.

All of those developments might still not have led to the industrial revolution had there not been a political revolution. The Meiji Restoration of 1868 brought to power new leadership from the old samurai class with a vision of a radically transformed country. Here again, to understand fully this new leadership and its receptivity to change and to new ideas, one must go back to the origins of the Tokugawa system and to the institutional developments that gradually changed the samurai from a rough, unlettered military class into a bureaucratic ruling elite. Because the samurai officialdom proved so responsive to the challenges of industrialization in the nineteenth century, Japan was able to pursue its modern goals without first enduring the kind of great internal upheaval that most other countries have suffered. A party within the old warrior elite seized power in 1868 and embarked upon a revolutionary program that saved Japan from national disaster, such as was experienced nearly everywhere else in Asia. Those warrior revolutionaries led Japan through a generation of reforms, which changed it from a predominantly agrarian society in 1868 to a nearly industrial economy by the turn of the century. An Englishman resident in Japan during this breathtaking change wrote that its swift pace "makes a man feel preternaturally old; for here he is in modern times, . . . and yet he can himself distinctly remember the Middle Ages. . . . Thus does it come about that . . . we ourselves feel well-nigh four hundred years old."

Japan's success in speedily expanding its national power was, however, purchased at a high cost in psychological strain and in human suffering. Driven by a peculiar combination of insecurity and ambition, the nation moved at a forced march in pursuit of industry and empire. All aspects of the society were subordinated to the national interest. Lafcadio Hearn, a sensitive observer of the stress Japan put itself under, wrote in 1894: "The nation has entered upon a period of intellectual overstrain. Consciously or unconsciously, in obedience to sudden necessity, Japan has undertaken nothing less than the tremendous task of forcing mental expansion up to the highest existing standard; and this means forcing the development of the nervous system. For the desired intellectual change, to be accomplished within a few generations, must involve a physiological change never to be effected without terrible cost. In other words, Japan has attempted too much; yet under the circumstances she could not have attempted less."[2] In 1911 the novelist Natsume Sōseki, despairing of the pace at which his country was driving itself, prophesied "nervous collapse" and admonished his countrymen not to be deluded into thinking of Japan as capable of competition on an equal footing with the great powers. The Christian writer Tokutomi Roka was likewise oppressed by a foreboding of disaster. He urged his country in 1906 to turn away from reliance on military power: "Awake, Japan, our beloved fatherland! Open your eyes and see your true self! Japan, repent!"

But historical circumstance did not make it easy for Japan to change course. Having been prodded to industrialize by the challenge of Western imperialism, Japan found its neighbors in East Asia governed by weak regimes in danger of collapse and of being taken over by the European empires, with consequent jeopardy to Japan's security and economic interests. Accordingly, a fear that China and Korea might fall under the sway of other countries, as well as ambition for equality with the Western imperial powers, drove Japan to territorial expansion.

To achieve those goals, Japan's leaders devised an ideology based on traditional social values of loyalty and solidarity and capable of mobilizing the entire nation. They relied on education, the media, the armed services, and a variety of government-sponsored organizations to instill and to mobilize support for the national goals at all levels of society. Industrialization and a vast empire were achieved, but in the course of their pursuit the ideology had continuously to be reinforced and to be inculcated more intensively in the populace, to overcome the recurring unrest in Japanese society caused by such taxing national ambitions. The ultimate price for what Lafcadio Hearn called the national "overstrain" was to blunder into a war that could not be won.

By the 1930s Japan had become virtually a prisoner of its own ideology. It was by no means the first time in history, nor was it the last, that a people was kept from pursuing its own best interests by the shortsighted and narrow way in which it conceived its national ideals. Japan lost nearly three million people in World War Two, including those first victims of the atomic age. The industry and empire for which it had striven were destroyed. The country was an international outcast, occupied by foreign soldiers for the first time in its history.

To dwell on Japan's "amazing success" in industrializing would, therefore, scarcely render accurately the nature of modern Japanese history. The new technology proved creative but also destructive; it offered new opportunities but at a high cost in human suffering and dislocation. Some students of modern Japan treat the militarist era of the 1930s and 1940s as an aberration, a temporary deviation from the path to becoming a modern industrial democracy. More reflection has led others, however, to point out that many of the same factors that promoted Japanese economic growth were also intrinsic to the rise of

2 The Writings of Lafcadio Hearn (Boston, 1923), VI, 367.

militaristic expansionism—in short, that industrialism and militarism were inextricably linked. Those who see the 1930s as an aberration take heart from the belief that the social democratic revolution induced by the American occupation has returned Japan to the proper path toward a modern progressive society. A more accurate perception of the nature of modern Japanese history may lie with those who take a less sanguine view of the course of contemporary world history: the view expressed, for example, by Reinhold Niebuhr, that "every technical advance, which previous generations regarded as a harbinger or guarantor of the redemption of mankind from its various difficulties, has proved to be the cause, or at least the occasion, for a new dimension of ancient perplexities."[3]

K.B.P.
August 1977

[3] Reinhold Niebuhr, *Faith and History* (New York, 1949), p. 1.

CONTENTS

PHOTOGRAPHS

MAPS

The first Europeans to arrive in Japan were Portuguese traders who landed on the island of Tanegashima off the southern coast in 1543. This first cultural confrontation between Japan and the West was a bewildering experience for both sides. As one observer at Tanegashima remarked whimsically of the Portuguese:

These men are traders. . . . They understand to a certain degree the distinction between Superior and Inferior, but I do not know whether they have a proper sense of ceremonial etiquette. They eat with their fingers instead of with chopsticks such as we use. They show their feelings without any self-control. They cannot understand the meaning of written characters. They are people who spend their lives roving hither and yon. They have no fixed abode and barter things which they have for those they do not, but withal they are a harmless sort of people.[1]

Jesuit missionaries began arriving in Japan in 1549 and as part of their proselytizing campaign made a genuine effort to understand Japanese manners and customs. It was no easy matter, and one Jesuit in exasperation finally concluded of the Japanese:

They have rites and ceremonies so different from those of all the other nations that it seems they deliberately try to be unlike any other people. The things which they do in this respect are beyond imagining and it may truly be said that Japan is a world the reverse of Europe; everything is so different and opposite that they are like us in practically nothing. . . . Now all this would not be

REUNIFICATION OF JAPAN

[1] Quoted in C. R. Boxer, *The Christian Century in Japan, 1549–1650* (Berkeley and Los Angeles, 1951), p. 29.

1

*surprising if they were like so many barbarians, but what aston-
ishes me is that they behave as very prudent and cultured people in all these matters.*[2]

As they became more familiar with the basic organization of
society and government, the Jesuits began to discern institutions
that were in many respects comparable to ones that had existed
in medieval Western Europe: a ruling class composed of military
leaders and their followers, practices of vassalage and enfeoff-
ment, a military code of honor, and the fragmentation of political
authority. Such similarities came to provide the basis for many
subsequent comparisons between the feudalism of Western
Europe and of Japan. Karl Marx pushed this comparison perhaps
as far as anyone else when he wrote in *Das Kapital:* "Japan,
with its purely feudal organization of landed property and its
developed *petite culture,* gives a much truer picture of the
European middle ages than our own history books. . . ."

The Warring States Period, 1467–1568

When the first Europeans arrived, Japan was in the midst of a
full-blown feudal period, marked by continuous, widespread
warfare. During this so-called "Warring States Period," which
lasted from the middle of the fifteenth to the middle of the
sixteenth centuries, power was fragmented to an extraordinary
degree. Not only had the authority of the central government
dissolved, but regional powerholders too had lost their positions.

Power, in short, lay at the local level. The most important
institution was the small feudal state dominated by the local
lord and his band of warriors (*samurai*). The lord's power was
based solely on his own military strength, for there were no
sources of security and prestige other than raw power. His
position depended on the continuing loyalty of his samurai
retainers, and thus he rewarded his leading vassals with fiefs,
titles, and other preferential treatment.

The normal state of relations among these small feudal
states was warfare. This was a period of great instability, and
fluctuations in power and in amounts of territory controlled
were continuous. If a lord failed to defend his territory he would

---

[2] Alessandro Valignano, quoted in Michael Cooper, *They Came to Japan*
(Berkeley and Los Angeles, 1965), p. 229.

either lose it to a more powerful neighboring lord or he would be overthrown by one of his own vassals.

Perhaps because betrayal and treachery were frequent, loyalty was the highest virtue. Yet no lord could wholly trust his vassals; they might try to overthrow him, or if they felt he was losing to a neighboring lord they might break away and join that lord. In these conditions of endemic warfare, lords were constantly suspicious of one another. It was not just that they were power mad, but rather, somewhat like nations in modern times, each one was afraid of his neighbor, fearful that if he himself did not expand, he would be conquered. The overriding concern of each lord, therefore, was to maximize his military power. This was a topsy-turvy age in which lords rose and fell not merely from one generation to another, but from one decade to another.

Power could scarcely have been further fragmented. Gradually, however, stabilizing forces began to appear. To overcome the conditions of upheaval and instability new institutions were created in the late 1500s, culminating in the establishment of the Tokugawa hegemony and the reunification of the country.

Consolidation of Local Power

The foundation for this great new unified order was laid in the second half of the sixteenth century with the consolidation of power at the local level. The primary reason for the new stability was the emergence, after a century of warfare, of feudal lords (daimyo) throughout the country who were able to impose greater control than their predecessors had over both their fighting men and the economic resources of the territory they controlled.

The local lord gained greater power vis-à-vis his samurai retainers by gradually diminishing the independent power bases that had existed within his domain. He learned that by obliging his vassals to reside close to him he could much more effectively control them. The lord achieved greater subordination of his warriors by organizing them more tightly into a methodical ranking. Similarly he was finding more systematic ways to assess the land tax on the peasantry in his domain.

As the process of consolidation of power at the local level went forward, a lord could associate himself with a more powerful lord in his region who would protect and guarantee his position. If then a lord's vassal rose against him, he could call on that powerful regional lord for help. In this way the daimyo formed regional groupings led by a particularly powerful lord; in turn, the power of each daimyo vis-à-vis his own vassals was enhanced by his belonging to such a grouping.

Castle Towns

This consolidation of power at the local level and the increased strength of the daimyo was dramatically symbolized by the massive castles they built in the latter half of the sixteenth century. In a relatively short space of time (especially in the period from 1580 to 1610) castles sprang up across the Japanese countryside. In all parts of the country the newly emergent daimyo, who numbered over two hundred, built great stone fortresses at the heart of their domains, where they could assemble their samurai retainers and effectively dominate the strategic and productive resources of the surrounding countryside.

These central citadels with towers soaring above the landscape symbolized the new ascendancy of the daimyo at the local level. To build the great structures they had to be able to mobilize large amounts of labor and to assemble highly skilled craftsmen. Previously, during the Warring States Period, fortifications had been of much smaller proportions and were ordinarily located on mountain tops, but in the new, more stable conditions castles were built in the lowlands and plains. Here, in and about the confines of the citadel, the lord settled his vassals and retainers.

As the warriors moved from the countryside into the castles, merchants and artisans and shrines and temples followed quickly to service the warriors' needs. Across Japan new "castle towns" came into being. Prior to 1550 nearly everyone had lived in farming and fishing villages. There were only two or three population centers that could accurately be called cities. One was Kyoto, the capital, which had about a quarter of a million inhabitants. Another was the nearby port of Sakai, the beneficiary of a flourishing overseas trade; it numbered perhaps 50,000 inhabitants. There were probably no more than a half dozen other towns with as many as 20,000. Edo (the present-day Tokyo) was still a fishing village.

Then with dramatic suddenness in the years after 1550 new cities began to spring up as a result of the increasing stability at the local level, the building of castles, and the withdrawal of samurai from the countryside. A period of extraordinary urban growth ensued. John W. Hall has written, "Most of the first-ranking castles and castle towns such as Himeji, Osaka,

Kanagawa, Wakayama, Tokushima, Kōchi, Takamatsu, Hiroshima, Edo, Wakamatsu, Okayama, Kōfu, Fushimi, Takasaki, Sendai, Fukuoka, Fukui, Kumamoto, Tottori, Matsuyama, Hikone, Fukushima, Yonezawa, Shizuoka, and Nagoya were founded during the brief span of years between 1580 and 1610. It would be hard to find a parallel period of urban construction in world history."[3] The castle towns became important urban centers in the various regions of Japan and remain so today. Edo grew into the modern metropolis of Tokyo. Two-thirds of the present prefectural capitals were once castle towns.

The building of those castle towns and the events associated with it, particularly the removal of most samurai from the countryside into the city, constitute one of the most important developments in the history of Japan. We may sum up their long-range significance in the following way:

1. The result of most immediate historical significance was that these fortresses and the control that they exercised over the local countryside further helped stabilize the local areas and provided the building blocks, the firm base upon which national unification could rest. With the samurai settled closely about the castle keep, the daimyo could the more easily control them and hence overcome the topsy-turvy nature of local politics that had prevailed during the preceding Warring States Period.

2. The gradual withdrawal of the samurai from the countryside set in motion a fundamental change in the nature of the warrior ruling class that had immense long-range significance for Japan. Previously samurai had been scattered over the land in villages, living on fiefs granted them by their lord, where they had been responsible for levying taxes, administering local justice, and keeping the peace. Now, however, living in a castle town, the warrior's ties with the land were soon cut. Instead of being rewarded with a fief from his lord, he was paid a stipend. Gradually, over the course of generations, the warriors ceased to be a landed elite. Instead they became more akin to bureaucrats, for the lord as he became absolute in his domain used his retainers as officials and clerks. Living in the castle town, with their juridical and social ties to the land gone, the warriors staffed the daimyo's bureaucracy. Thomas C. Smith sums up the profound transformation that was taking place:

The lord, having taken in his hands his vassals' political and judicial functions, now governed an average population of about

[3] John W. Hall, "The Castle Town and Japan's Modern Urbanization," in J. W. Hall and M. B. Jansen (eds.), *Studies in the Institutional History of Early Modern Japan* (Princeton, 1968), p. 176. Copyright © 1968 by Princeton University Press; Princeton Paperback, 1970. Reprinted by permission of Princeton University Press.

100,000. To police so large a population, to collect its taxes and regulate its trade, to give it justice and maintain its roads and irrigation works, required a small army of officials and clerks. The lord, of course, used his vassals to perform these functions, to man the expanding and differentiating bureaucracy under him. The warriors who manned the bureaucracy exercised far more power over the rest of the population than warriors ever had before; but it was a new kind of power. Formerly power was personal and territorial; it pertained to a piece of land and belonged to a man as inherited right. Now it was impersonal and bureaucratic: it pertained to a specialized office to which one must be appointed and from which he might be removed.[4]

As the warrior's legal relationship to the land changed, as he became more akin to a bureaucratic officeholder, he came to lack private economic or political power. This fact had great historical significance. The gradual transformation of the feudal ruling class into a landless bureaucratic elite helps to explain the remarkable responsiveness of Japan in the nineteenth century. When faced with the challenge of undertaking the great political and economic changes required by the industrial revolution, Japan responded quickly, in part because it had no politically powerful landed class, no entrenched land-based gentry such as existed in China, which would bitterly resist those changes. We shall explore this factor more later. Here it is sufficient to point out that the movement of samurai from the countryside to the castle town in the sixteenth and seventeenth centuries radically changed the nature of the ruling class, in a way that was to ease economic and political change in the nineteenth century.

3. Another consequence associated with the appearance of castle towns and the consolidation of local power was the development of local administrative practice. As the Warring States Period gave way to peaceful stability in the seventeenth century, the castle towns became concerned less with military matters than with problems of local administration. As Hall has summed up: "The great castles of Japan came to house the central and local administrative headquarters of the nation. From them political authority radiated outward into the countryside. . . . Life in Tokugawa Japan became infinitely more regularized and subject to written law than under earlier feudal regimes, and this in turn was a step in the direction of more modern public administration."[5]

[4] Thomas C. Smith, "Japan's Aristocratic Revolution," *Yale Review*, L, 3 (1961), p. 375. Copyright © Yale University.
[5] Hall, in Hall & Jansen, pp. 179, 183. Reprinted by permission of Princeton University Press.

4. The growth of the castle towns helped bring into being a large and vital merchant class during the Tokugawa Period (1600–1868). As samurai gradually settled around the castle, a merchant class to service them sprang up. The emerging castle town became the economic center of its domain. As time went on, the merchants took on greater importance and the samurai depended on them to fulfill vital economic functions. One contemporary Confucianist, lamenting the growing power of the merchants, wrote that the samurai in towns lived "as if in an inn"—dependent on the services of the merchants.

5. Along with the rise of the mercantile class, there was a gradual growth during the Tokugawa Period of a market economy and of specialization and commercialization in agriculture. In place of the old self-sufficient pattern, farming tended to become far more specialized as produce was sold in the local market. The peasants more and more grew the special crops for which their climate and land were best suited. What they did not themselves produce, they could buy. One must be careful not to exaggerate the suddenness of this development: it took place gradually over a long period of time and at a different pace in various parts of the country.

6. The growth of castle towns contributed to the improvement of transportation. Roads to and from the castle towns became essential for economic, administrative, and strategic functions.

7. Castle towns contributed to development of an urban culture. The brightest and gaudiest culture existed in Edo and Osaka, but even the smaller castle towns were infected by the tastes and life style of the townsmen.

In tracing the long-range significance of the castle towns, we have gotten far ahead of our story, for these results unfolded gradually over the course of the Tokugawa Period and were by no means evident in the late sixteenth century when castle towns came into being. We shall pursue each one of these consequences in greater detail in the succeeding pages.

Toward Unification

The stabilization of power at the local level made available the firm base upon which first regional and then national unity could be built. Gradually daimyo at the regional level joined together, the lesser daimyo pledging loyalty to or being conquered by the strongest daimyo in the region. In warfare that occupied the years from 1570 to 1600 these regional groupings contended with one another for national hegemony. It was three successive daimyo from central Honshu who assembled a powerful coalition of forces, one by one gained the submission of other regional clusters of daimyo, and ultimately succeeded in unifying Japan.

These three lords were Oda Nobunaga (1534–1582), his chief vassal Toyotomi Hideyoshi (1536–1598), and Toyotomi's vassal Tokugawa Ieyasu (1542–1616). What enabled these three extraordinary men to bring about a new centralization of power? Partly their success was due to their strategic location in central Honshu, where they could control the greatest food-producing plains in Japan and where they had easy access to Kyoto, the capital and traditional symbol of legitimacy for national political power. Partly it was the result of brilliant military strategy. No less important, however, was their demonstrated mastery of two of the main sources of feudal power that had to be controlled and exploited: land and peasants.

Osaka castle, built in 1583 by Toyotomi Hideyoshi. *Courtesy of Consulate General of Japan, N.Y.*

Toyotomi Hideyoshi, who succeeded to leadership of the reunification campaign after Oda's death in 1582, was particularly successful in devising measures to strengthen control of the land and peasants under his sway. In the 1580s he ordered a sweeping resurvey of the cultivated land in the countryside to determine the productivity of each piece of land and identify the individual responsible for paying the tax on it. Not only did the land survey tighten collection of the land tax and provide a solid new basis for village organization; in addition it allowed Toyotomi to assign to his vassal daimyo lands he had conquered with firm knowledge of the value of those lands. At the same time he carried out his so-called "sword hunt" by an edict that forbade all non-samurai to keep "swords, sidearms, daggers, spears or any other military equipment." Thus a sharp line of distinction was drawn between the sword-carrying warrior elite and the disarmed commoners. Other edicts sought to freeze society by tying peasants to their villages and occupation. Similarly, samurai were not to return to the villages, nor were they to change masters. Toyotomi's purpose was to eliminate both physical and occupational mobility and to stabilize the social order.

These reforms, occurring as the castle towns were being built throughout Japan, served to enhance the trend toward consolidation of the daimyo's power. The meticulous land survey made it easier to withdraw samurai from the countryside and supervise the tax collection from the castle. The other reforms, which disarmed the commoners and tied them to their occupation and village, made local society more tractable to daimyo rule. Thus, as the coalition of daimyo led by Toyotomi gradually brought the country under its authority, reforms were instituted that strengthened the daimyo vis-à-vis their retainers and that diminished the possibility of disruption at the local level. The basis was laid for the remarkable national social and political order that would endure over two and a half centuries.

Toyotomi Hideyoshi's death in 1598 occasioned an intense two-year power struggle to determine who among the most powerful daimyo should succeed him as overlord of the land. At a decisive battle fought in October 1600 at Sekigahara, near Kyoto, the coalition of daimyo forces led by Tokugawa Ieyasu triumphed over an alliance of daimyo from western Japan. He emerged in a pre-eminent position, able to dispose of all those daimyo who would not accept his overlordship and in possession of an immense amount of territory acquired as the spoils of war, which he could divide among his loyal followers.

From this position of strength the Tokugawa family spent the next several decades building a new system of government. This was accomplished by institutionalizing the control measures devised by themselves and their predecessors during the march toward national unification. It is extremely important to grasp the basic outlines of this system because it provided the framework of Japanese politics and society from which modern Japan emerged.

The Tokugawa Bakufu

In 1603 Tokugawa Ieyasu was invested by the Emperor with the position of *shogun* (generalissimo), traditionally the highest military office in the land. Although in reality Ieyasu's position depended entirely on his own military power, since he had fought his way to the top of the feudal hierarchy, Ieyasu made much of his investiture: the Emperor, although without real political power or even much private wealth, was regarded as the source of political legitimacy, the locus of sovereignty, and the symbol of national unity. In the seventh and eighth centuries, when the Chinese imperial model had been adopted by the Japanese and the

ESTABLISHMENT OF THE TOKUGAWA SYSTEM

capital was established first at Nara and then at Kyoto, the prestige and influence of the imperial family were at their zenith. Even in that time, however, a tradition of the Emperor reigning but not ruling was beginning to take root. Over the next centuries, political power slipped into the hands of the Kyoto nobility and then, as the central government declined, into the hands of feudal fighting men in the countryside. But even as power fragmented and Japan entered a period of full-blown feudalism, the old imperial system, centered in Kyoto, remained the source of legitimacy. The Tokugawa were careful to observe this tradition, not only by seeking to be appointed shogun by the Emperor, but also by acquiring court titles and establishing family ties with the nobility—and ultimately with the imperial house itself. Thus Tokugawa Ieyasu and his descendants who succeeded him as shogun were technically appointed officials, holding the civil and military functions of government delegated by the Emperor.

While these lines of legitimacy were established through the old imperial system in Kyoto, the reality of Tokugawa power depended on stabilizing the coalition of daimyo through which national unification had been achieved. Ieyasu established his seat of government in Edo (present-day Tokyo), where his new castle was built. Government by the shogun, often referred to as the shogunate or *bakufu* (a term meaning military government), was an extremely complex and intricate mechanism. Basically the shogun administered the country along two lines.

First, roughly one-quarter of the land belonged directly to the Tokugawa family, amassed during their rise to power. These lands, scattered throughout the countryside but mostly concentrated in central Honshu, the Tokugawa administered directly through their own samurai retainers. In this category of direct Tokugawa rule were all the important mines, the major seaports, including Osaka and Nagasaki, and the old capital city of Kyoto. Within these direct holdings the bakufu raised its funds, and its rule was in every way absolute.

Second, the remainder of the country, approximately three-quarters of it, was governed indirectly through the daimyo, all of whom after 1600 swore allegiance to the Tokugawa. It was this second, indirect mechanism of governing the country that gave the Tokugawa their greatest concern. Here their power was by no means absolute; it depended on maintaining the coalition of daimyo. Among the daimyo there were some who were very powerful, and the possibility of an anti-Tokugawa alliance among them was an ever-present danger. Because the Tokugawa were not strong enough fully to subjugate the daimyo, the latter were left largely autonomous within their own domains. The bakufu regulated the external affairs of the daimyo's domain but refrained from interfering in internal affairs so long as the daimyo gave no sign of disloyalty toward the Tokugawa.

During the two and a half centuries of Tokugawa rule, the number of daimyo varied between 240 and 295. A daimyo was officially defined as a lord possessing a *han* (domain) with an assessed productivity of at least 10,000 *koku* of rice (1 koku = 4.96 bushels). The size of daimyo domains varied considerably; the largest was assessed at over a million koku.

There were three different categories of daimyo:

1. The *shimpan* (related) daimyo were members of Tokugawa branch families. Should the main line of the family die out, a shogun would be chosen from among these lords, who came to number 23.

2. The *fudai* (hereditary) daimyo were those who had pledged loyalty to the Tokugawa prior to the decisive battle of Sekigahara in 1600. Because their loyalty preceded this decisive battle, they were generally considered trustworthy and they helped staff the central councils of the shogunate. By the eighteenth century they numbered in the neighborhood of 140 daimyo.

3. The *tozama* (outer) daimyo were those who had taken Tokugawa Ieyasu as their overlord only after the battle of Sekigahara. Because their pledge of loyalty was relatively recent, they were generally regarded as less trustworthy and therefore excluded from positions in the shogunate. Indeed, among the outer daimyo were lords who had fought against the Tokugawa coalition at Sekigahara, the two most important of which were the domains of Satsuma and Chōshū. Although they had submitted to the Tokugawa after Sekigahara, they still could not be trusted and had to be kept under constant surveillance. (Eventually, two and a half centuries later, it was those two domains that led the overthrow of the shogunate.) Not all of the outer lords had traditions hostile to the Tokugawa. Kaga domain, for example, had been allied with the Tokugawa at Sekigahara, though it had not yet taken Ieyasu as overlord. Many of the outer daimyo possessed very large domains. Kaga was officially assessed at over a million koku, Satsuma at 770,000, and Chōshū at 369,000. (Lands held directly by the Tokugawa were assessed at over 7,000,000 koku.) The outer lords numbered in the neighborhood of 100.

Tokugawa Control System

To maintain hegemony over this unwieldy feudal coalition, the Tokugawa depended on various control measures:

1. *Rearrangement of domains.* One of the most important control measures was the power the shogun had to rearrange or reassign landed holdings for strategic reasons. In this way the disposition of fiefs could be arranged so that potentially disloyal daimyo would be shunted to remote positions or hedged in by loyal daimyo.

2. *Alternate attendance system.* By far the most important method devised for controlling the daimyo was what was called the system of alternate attendance. Under this system all daimyo were obliged to alternate their residence periodically between their domains and Edo. Ordinarily this meant residing in Edo every other year. While they were in Edo, the shogunate could maintain surveillance over them. When they returned to their domains, the daimyo were required to leave behind their wives and children as hostages. In theory, sojourns in Edo were arranged so that about half the daimyo would be in attendance at any particular time.

Surveillance was not the only purpose. The system also served as a continuous drain on the economic resources of the daimyo. They had to build and maintain houses in Edo for their families and retainers, a considerable number of whom accompanied them on their biennial trip. While in Edo the daimyo were required to perform certain types of ceremonies as well as guard duty. The bakufu made periodic levies for money and labor. A daimyo who gave the appearance of becoming too powerful or who in some other way was offensive to the bakufu might be instructed to repair a castle, a shrine, or a bridge. It became common for daimyo to spend over half of their domains' tax income for the costs of the alternate attendance system.

3. *Seclusion.* A third measure designed in part to control the daimyo was the isolation of Japan. This policy was designed to cut off the lords—particularly the powerful outer lords—from the military and economic sources of strength that foreign trade might offer them. It was also intended to eliminate Christianity as a source of social disruption in the stable order the Tokugawa were trying to establish. The Jesuits in their earlier efforts had succeeded, according to their own estimates, in making hundreds of thousands of converts. How meaningful these estimates are is difficult to say, but they did have some successes. Perhaps what was most disturbing to the Tokugawa was the conversion of several important daimyo. Measures to limit the activities of Western missionaries had already been initiated under Toyotomi Hideyoshi. Under the Tokugawa those measures became more stringent: all missionaries were expelled, converts forced to recant, and fiendish persecutions sanctioned. By 1650 Christianity was almost completely eliminated.

An early seventeenth-century Japanese portrayal of a European ship arriving. *Courtesy of the Museum of Fine Arts, Boston, Fenollosa-Weld Collection*

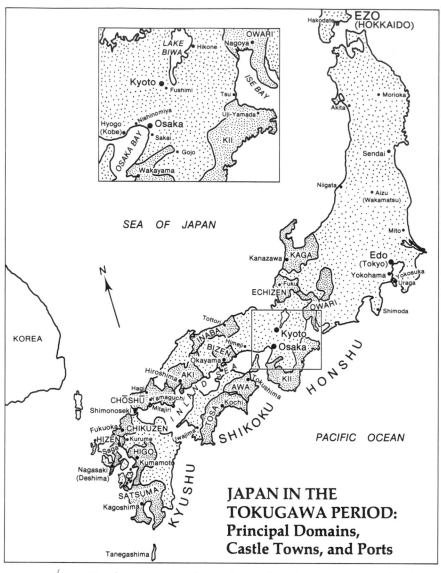

JAPAN IN THE TOKUGAWA PERIOD: Principal Domains, Castle Towns, and Ports

Trade, too, was brought under the tight control of the shogunate. Prior to 1600 there had been strong indications of a quickening expansionist impulse. There had been a growth of commercial ties with other parts of East and Southeast Asia; most notably, Toyotomi Hideyoshi with grandiose plans of empire had made an abortive invasion of the Korean peninsula in the 1590s. This expansionist urge, however, had to be suppressed, for the requirements of social stability were paramount.

By three exclusion decrees issued in the 1630s, ties with the outside world were almost entirely severed. Japanese were prohibited from traveling abroad and the size of ships being built was limited to that necessary for coastal trade within the Japanese archipelago. All trade with Western countries was ended except for commercial ties with the Dutch, who were permitted a small trading station on the tiny island of Deshima in the harbor of Nagasaki. Here the Dutch merchants were virtually prisoners, free only to walk up and down the two streets of their island, watched, guarded, and spied upon. Somewhat like the daimyo, the Dutch were compelled to make periodic trips to Edo to pay their respects to the shogun.

Englebert Kaempfer, a German doctor serving with the Dutch trading station, described the ludicrous audiences with the shogun (whom he mistakenly called "the Emperor") in 1691:

As soon as the [head of the trading company] came thither, [the attendants] cried aloud Hollanda Captain which was the signal for him to draw near and make his obeisance. Accordingly he crawled on his hands and knees to a place showed him between the presents, ranged in due order on one side, and the place where the Emperor [Shogun!] sat on the other, and then, kneeling, he bowed his forehead quite down to the ground, and so crawled backwards like a crab, without uttering one single word. . . . The mutual compliments being over, the succeeding part of this solemnity turned to a perfect farce. We were asked a thousand ridiculous and impertinent questions. The Emperor . . . ordered us to take off our cappas, or cloaks, being our garments of ceremony; then to stand upright that he might have a full view of us; again to walk, to stand still, to compliment each other, to dance, to jump, to play the drunkard, to speak broken Japanese, to read Dutch, to paint, to sing, to put our cloaks on and off. Meanwhile we obeyed the Emperor's commands in the best manner we could, I joining to my dance a love-song in High German. In this manner and with innumerable such other apish tricks, we must suffer ourselves to contribute to the Emperor's and the Court's diversion.[1]

Aside from the limited commercial contacts with the Dutch, some trade was also carried on with China, Korea, and the Ryukyus. For the most part, however, during the next two centuries Japanese society developed in almost complete isolation.

4. *Ideology.* A fourth control directed primarily at the daimyo and their retainers was the use of ideology. Neo-Confucian doctrines were given official sanction by the shogunate as a means of providing a philosophical foundation for the new

[1] Englebert Kaempfer, *History of Japan* (Glasgow, 1906), pp. 295–297.

social and political order taking shape. Confucianism was not new in Japan. It had been introduced centuries earlier but it had never been so appropriate as it now became. Confucianism held up familial relations as a proper model for government, relations between parent and child being analogous to those between ruler and subject. Since political authority derived its legitimacy from its ethical basis, the ruling elite must by their exemplary moral conduct set an example for the rest of society. Social distinctions were held to be in the natural order of things, and each class, each age, each group had to fulfill its obligations and maintain its proper place if society was to preserve harmony. In sum, Tokugawa society promised to be much more ordered, settled, and regulated than earlier times; and Confucian concepts of a hierarchical society in accord with nature, of benevolent paternalism in government, of an ethical basis for administration, and of a meritorious officialdom, all coincided with Tokugawa purposes.

In addition to the above controls, various other measures were taken to regulate the activities of the daimyo. Many of them were codified. These directives regulated contacts between daimyo, the contracting of marriages between daimyo families, the repair of castles, and the like. Barriers were established on the main highways to monitor the comings and goings of daimyo and their retainers. A system of passports provided further means to check on travel.

Government at the Domain Level

Within their own domains, or *han* as they came to be called later, the daimyo were left with a great deal of autonomy, free from interference so long as they did not behave in any way regarded as disloyal by the shogunate. The daimyo paid no taxes to the shogunate, although they were subject to periodic exactions of money and labor. Within the han a daimyo was absolute. His position was hereditary, passing ordinarily to his eldest son. When there was no heir, one was adopted. In practice, because the daimyo spent much of his time in Edo, his leading vassals often tended to exercise actual administrative leadership in the han.

The samurai class constituted 6 or 7 percent of the population and alone had the right to wear swords and to assume a family surname. It would be a mistake, however, to think of the warriors as a homogeneous group, for there was a great deal of spread or differential within the class. Warriors ranged from the shogun and daimyo at the top, down to the foot soldiers at the bottom. The high-ranking warriors served on the Council of Elders, or in some other capacity as advisors to the daimyo. They also acted as heads of guard groups or standing army units, as chiefs of police, as supervisors of financial affairs, and as liaison agents between the daimyo and the shogunate. The middle ranks of samurai served in bureaucratic posts having to do with administration of the castle town, the collection of taxes, and the management of religious and educational affairs. They may also have headed various lesser units of the militia. At the lower levels, warriors served as clerks or as low-ranking military men.

There was thus a minute gradation of hierarchy within the samurai class, with great differences between top and bottom. In Chōshū, for example, Albert Craig tells us that among the 5,675 direct vassals of the daimyo there were 40 different ranks. This differential in status was reflected in the annual rice stipend warriors were paid, as the tabulation shows.[2]

Income (koku)	Number of families in the group
Over 100	661
Over 70 and less than 100	202
Over 50 and less than 70	339
Over 40 and less than 50	472
Under 40	4,001
Total	5,675

Consciousness of rank and observance of status distinctions were maintained throughout society. At the domain school for sons from samurai families in Kaga—to give one interesting example—R. P. Dore tells us that regulations provided that any boy from the highest-ranking families was permitted to come to school accompanied by two retainers, as well as one servant to take care of his sandals during school hours and another to hold his umbrella on rainy days. Children from the next rank "could have one retainer, a sandal-minder, and an umbrella-holder. The next, one retainer and a sandal-minder, but they should carry their own umbrella. Younger sons, and those of the lowest

[2] Tabulation from Albert Craig, *Chōshū in the Meiji Restoration* (Cambridge, Mass., 1961), p. 113. Copyright © 1961 by the President and Fellows of Harvard College. Used by permission of Harvard University Press.

rank, should come without servants; the school would provide someone to look after their sandals *en masse.*"[3]

The educator Fukuzawa Yukichi, writing in 1877 after the destruction of the Tokugawa system, looked back with loathing at the status distinctions that were observed in speech, dress, and daily intercourse:

An ashigaru *[foot soldier] always had to prostrate himself on the ground in the presence of an upper samurai. If he should encounter an upper samurai on the road in the rain, he had to take off his* geta *[clogs] and prostrate himself by the roadside. . . . Upper samurai rode on horseback, lower samurai went on foot. Upper samurai possessed the privileges of hunting wild boar and fishing; lower samurai had no such privileges. . . . The broad distinction between the upper and lower classes was, however, accepted unquestioningly, almost as though it were a law of nature rather than an invention of man.*[4]

Village Government

As a result of the withdrawal of the warriors from the countryside into the castle towns, the actual administration of peasant villages fell into the hands of village headmen. The lord appointed from among his vassals supervisors who would oversee the work of headmen. But within the village itself there was considerable autonomy. Each village, led by its headman, was largely self-governing, and the daimyo would not interfere so long as order was maintained and the taxes were paid to the lord.

The headman came from among the peasants themselves—generally from the old, prestigious, and wealthy families in the village. In many villages the position was hereditary; in others the office was rotated among leading families in the village; and occasionally the headman was elected by propertied villagers. He was responsible for keeping records, settling disputes, maintaining order, and above all for apportioning and collecting the tax that was levied on the village. Often he operated with the help of a village assembly and village codes. By allowing the headman certain visible symbols of status, such as elegant clothing

[3] Ronald P. Dore, *Education in Tokugawa Japan* (Berkeley and Los Angeles, 1965), pp. 181–182.
[4] Fukuzawa Yukichi, "Kyūhanjō," Carmen Blacker (trans.), in *Monumenta Nipponica* 9 (1953), pp. 310–311. Used by permission.

and housing, the lord encouraged the peasants to respect and look up to the headman. The typical village was made up of between fifteen and forty clustered houses and was characterized by a strong sense of solidarity, encouraged by centuries of close living and by the cooperative nature of farming. The conformity of everyone in the village to group sentiment was usually assured by a variety of social pressures, not the least important of which was gossip. The successful headman governed by building up a consensus; and disputes within the village were generally settled by conciliation, compromise, and patient negotiation, in which the headman played the leading role.

The Tokugawa leaders set out to create institutions that would stabilize political and social conditions in the country and thereby prevent a breakup of their coalition and a lapse back into feudal warfare. They succeeded remarkably well. Isolated for the most part from the rest of the world, the Tokugawa system endured until 1868. During this period there were very few battles to be fought: the Warring States Period had given way to an era of ordered living. The control measures, instituted to preserve the balance of forces within the coalition that brought the Tokugawa to power, proved effective in inhibiting political change.

Society, while stable, did not remain static. Although on the surface the Tokugawa political system held intact for over two and a half centuries, the entire social and economic basis of that system was quietly transformed. All classes of Japanese —warriors, peasants, merchants—underwent profound change in nature and structure. Tokugawa society grew in unexpected directions until at last a political revolution was inevitable.

Roots of Change

The very success of the Tokugawa system was in the long run responsible for its undoing. Paradoxically, the roots of revolutionary economic and social change lay in the very reforms just discussed, which were carried out in the sixteenth and seventeenth centuries to try to stabilize society. The control measures, especially the alternate attendance system and the removal of samurai from the countryside, effectively maintained the political status quo, but at the same time they promoted economic changes that slowly undermined the Tokugawa order.

The isolation of the nation might have been expected to retard economic growth, for

GROWTH OF TOKUGAWA SOCIETY

3

several of the flourishing cities, such as the ports of Sakai and Hakata, had depended upon foreign trade. The economy now turned in upon itself. It might have stagnated except that the requirements of the Tokugawa system provided a powerful stimulant to new economic activity.

Consider the alternate attendance system. Inadvertently, it was surely one of the most important factors contributing to the rise of a money economy. It was intended as a means to control the daimyo by requiring their periodic attendance at the capital, where the bakufu could keep them under continuous surveillance; by requiring the maintenance of residences in Edo, where families were kept as hostages to deter rebellion; finally, by draining their finances by the heavy cost of journeying to and from the capital and of maintaining residences there.

The expenses of the daimyo for the periodic (ordinarily biennial) sojourns in Edo were very great. The largest of the daimyo proceeded to the capital with as many as several thousand retainers; and costs for food and lodging, for hiring boats and porters to cross the numerous water barriers, and the like became immense. As tastes grew more luxurious the processions became occasions for competitive display. Weapons and equipage were elaborately and expensively decorated, thereby advertising the status of the daimyo. In the capital, consumption tended to be even more conspicuous. Each daimyo normally had several mansions, maintained by a permanent staff which, in the case of the largest daimyo, numbered over 10,000 in the middle of the eighteenth century.

To obtain specie for these enormous expenses, a daimyo took a large portion of the tax rice collected from the peasantry in his domain and sold it in Osaka and other market centers. Subsequent use of specie stimulated the growth of commercial transactions and an increased use of money. In Edo (not to mention along the main roads leading into the capital) businesses sprang up to cater to the wants of the warriors and to serve the needs of a growing population. Of negligible size before the battle of Sekigahara, Edo grew to a metropolis of about one million by 1720—considerably larger than London or Paris at that time. Teeming with samurai visiting from all parts of the country, it became Japan's chief consumption center. To the southwest Osaka, the chief market for surplus rice of many han, also became a great distribution center, with a powerful merchant class directing its commercial activity. Although it grew less rapidly than Edo, by 1800 Osaka had a population of 400,000, and taken together with nearby Kyoto and Sakai the area comprised an urban population in the neighborhood of a million people. Much of the trade of the country converged on the Edo and the Osaka-Kyoto areas.

So the alternate attendance system achieved its purpose of maintaining the political status quo only for a time. In the long run it undermined the political order by stimulating fundamental economic and social change that the Tokugawa system could not accommodate.

In addition to the alternate attendance system, the removal of the samurai from the countryside and their settlement in the castle towns also had ironic and unexpected results in the long run. The original purpose, as we have seen, sprang from the daimyo's determination to diminish the "independence" of his vassals and thereby stabilize the political system at the domain level. But the settlement of samurai in the castle towns created local consumption centers and brought into being a merchant class that was of considerable size and influence. A market system grew up to supply the wants of the samurai class and in the long run came to occupy a position of great economic importance. At the same time, the growth of a market network around the castle towns fundamentally altered the social order in the countryside. What had been intended as a measure to control the lord's retainers ended by contributing to a vast change in local society.

Transformation of the Samurai Class

The new circumstances of society also immensely changed the nature of the samurai class. As warfare ceased to be a way of life and a sedentary style took its place, the samurai were compelled to adjust to conditions of peace. In essence their transformation was from a feudal military class to a bureaucratic elite, and though warrior traditions were kept alive, the reality of their daily life had little in common with that of their predecessors in the Warring States Period.

Living in the castle towns on stipends paid them by their lord, the warriors manned his expanding and rapidly differentiating bureaucracy. Rules were established, regularizing their behavior in patterns befitting bureaucrats. Codes were issued, standardizing bureaucratic procedure by providing rules for office hours, for procurement and purchase of office supplies, for systems of guard duty, and other like subjects. Gradually the foundations of civil administration were laid, as the daimyo promulgated codes regulating many aspects of political and economic life and as he clarified procedures of government and chains of administrative responsibility. By the end of the seventeenth century, the daimyo's government had become a complex and elaborately structured bureaucratic organization with a finely graded officialdom that had charge of rural, town, financial, temple and shrine, and social affairs.

Under the peaceful conditions that prevailed, effective governance depended upon an orderly civil administration and the rule of public law. The lord therefore had very different expectations of his retainers than was the case earlier. One lord, writing in 1714, "lamented the tendency of officials to ignore administrative precedent; henceforth, he states, they should consult the office diaries kept by predecessors and conduct all business accordingly, calling this strict observance of precedent the 'highest loyalty'."[1] To samurai of the Warring States Period such a conception of loyalty would have been unimaginable!

The contradictions between their living martial traditions, symbolized by the two swords they wore, and the new position of samurai as a civil administrative elite were not easy to reconcile. The most dramatic illustration of this tension occurred when 47 masterless samurai (rōnin) determined to avenge the death of their lord in accord with the traditional warrior code. Their vendetta, however, transgressed shogunal law, and after anguished controversy—in which they were praised in some quarters for their high ideals and condemned in others for their illegal behavior—they were at last required to commit seppuku (ritual suicide).

Confucian scholars, writing on the code of the warrior (bushidō), sought to reconcile these tensions by urging the samurai to strike a balance between military training and book learning. The latter, however, tended to loom larger in the warrior's new role as civil administrator. One of the most interesting and important aspects of the transformation was the increasing literacy and education of the samurai. At the beginning of the Tokugawa Period warriors were a rough, unlettered class, but by the end nearly all were literate and schooled. From the outset Tokugawa Ieyasu stressed that pursuit of learning must be given the same consideration as the military arts. Learning was necessary in order to acquire the practical techniques of operating a bureaucracy as well as the moral principles upon which samurai government was founded.

Rule by a hereditary military elite was justified with the assertion that samurai governed by virtue of their ethical ex-

[1] Thomas C. Smith, "The Discontented," *Journal of Asian Studies*, XXI, 2 (1962), p. 215.

ample. Therefore study of the Confucian classics was essential. The bakufu led the way in educational development by establishing a Confucian academy in Edo early in the period, and the domains followed this example by also founding schools in the castle towns. Domain-sponsored schools proliferated in the latter half of the Tokugawa Period and by the end there were nearly two hundred.

Change in Agrarian Society

At the outset of the Tokugawa Period a pattern of self-sufficient, cooperative farming prevailed over nearly all the countryside. Consciousness of individual and class interests tended to be submerged in the cohesiveness and solidarity of village society. Physical isolation and the rudimentary state of the market imposed a self-sufficiency whereby the typical village produced simply what it needed to feed and cloth its own members and to pay the land tax in kind. If there was any surplus it was stored away for future use in time of crop failure and famine. There was very little occasion to buy and sell.

The nature of the Tokugawa system transformed this pattern of farming; rural life began to change markedly, especially by the eighteenth century. As cities grew and communications improved, the peasant began to find a market to dispose of whatever surplus goods he produced. In addition to the great urban centers of Edo and Osaka, there were the new castle towns scattered across the countryside, and nearly every village was within reach of those growing population centers. Villages were thereby drawn into market networks that soon changed both their pattern of farming and their structure of social relations.

Commercial farming spread rapidly and widely during the Tokugawa Period. Villages began to grow crops that would fill the needs of the cities and towns; they began to specialize in the crops that their soil, climate, and market favored. Those necessities that they no longer produced could be purchased in the nearby market. Regional specialization in commercial crops therefore steadily increased: the Osaka area became famous for its mandarin oranges, cotton products, and fish fertilizers; central Honshu was known for its cultivation of mulberries and raising of silkworms; sugar cane was grown mainly in Kyushu; Shikoku produced paper, salt, and lumber. Small village enterprises such as sugar, salt, tea, oil, sericulture, and textile industries spread rapidly, as in fact did more substantial forms of rural enterprise, including the production of wine, soy sauce, ceramics, and iron. Peasants found in these rural industries sidelines to supplement their farm incomes.

With the commercialization of agriculture, the use of money spread. Buying and selling became a common aspect of village life. How commercial rural Japan had become by the end of the Tokugawa Period is suggested by the economic historian Sydney Crawcour. He estimates that "over half and probably nearer two-thirds of output" in Japanese agriculture was marketed in one form or another. He cites a village shopkeeper in an economically advanced area of western Japan who as early as 1813 was selling "the following impressive list of commodities: ink, paper, writing brushes, *herasaki*, cauldrons, cutlery, needles, smoking pipes, tobacco, tobacco pouches, teapots, casserole dishes, rice-wine bottles, oil containers, vinegar, soy sauce, bean paste, salt, matting, noodles, kelp, hair oil, hair strings, hairpins, cotton cloth, socks, towels, bamboo trellis, carrying baskets, zōri [thongs], straw sandals, wooden clogs, tea, teacups, lucifers [matches], wicks, incense, fire pots, lanterns, oil, candles, rice wine, timber, hot water bottles, cakes, *sembei* [crackers], trays, funeral requisites, grain, *and other everyday necessities*"![2]

With the rising productivity in the countryside there went an increase in the average standard of living, but it was by no means evenly divided among the peasants. The farming class was every bit as stratified as the others. Most noticeable was the emergence of a class of wealthy peasants (*gōnō*), who clearly benefited the most from the commercialization of the agrarian economy. It was on their land that the greatest increases in productivity usually occurred, for they could afford better fertilizers and improved farm implements. They used their growing wealth to invest in the widely spreading rural industries—*sake* (rice wine) brewing, dyeing, silk and cotton weaving, and the like. Still another outlet for gōnō wealth was money lending, which permitted them to foreclose on mortgaged land in times of general economic distress and thereby to become large landholders.

Concentration of landownership and the spread of tenant farming was very noticeable in many of the more economically advanced sections of the country during the late Tokugawa Period. In many villages landless peasants constituted a significant group. The development of the market economy was bringing about new class relations in the village, as the cooperative

[2] E. Sydney Crawcour, "The Tokugawa Heritage," in W. W. Lockwood (ed.), *The State and Economic Enterprise in Japan* (Princeton, 1965), p. 41.

nature of farming and the cohesiveness of the village declined. One result of this growing consciousness of the disparity of wealth in the villages was a sharp increase in the number of peasant uprisings in the last century of Tokugawa rule—a subject to which we shall turn in the next chapter.

Finally, we should not leave the topic of change in the countryside without noting one of the most intriguing aspects of the Tokugawa Period, that is, the leveling off in the rate of population increase after a sharp rise in the seventeenth century. It used to be thought that population was held in check by disease, famine, and other natural disasters and the consequent resort to infanticide and abortion. Recent studies, however, suggest that the population stability characteristic of the late Tokugawa Period was more the result of social controls designed to limit the size of families and the number of households within a village than it was of desperation and social demoralization. A village case study directed by Thomas Smith finds, for example, that infanticide was practiced by "the most respectable and stable part of the population" in order to achieve "overall family limitation, an equilibrium of some sort between family size and farm size; [and] an advantageous distribution of the sexes in children. . . ."[3] Such behavior bespeaks a surprising foresight and "rationality"—an attitudinal change that may well have conduced to Japan's subsequent industrialization. In fact, two scholars of this problem have concluded that "Tokugawa Japan as a whole was clearly not trapped in a low-level economic equilibrium with a high rate of population growth ready to sap whatever surplus the economy was able to generate. . . . In short, the pre-industrial population and economic development of Japan can be compared most readily with that of England. Japan like England, experienced a rate of population increase well under one half of 1 percent per annum, while output increased steadily at a higher rate."[4]

We may sum up our discussion of change in agrarian society during the Tokugawa period by pointing out how recent scholarship has revised our view of the countryside. Traditional scholarship tended to stress the plight of the peasantry, its exploitation by the other classes, the oppressive rate of taxation, the increase of tenancy, and the corresponding concentration of

[3] Robert Y. Eng and Thomas C. Smith, "Peasant Families and Population Control in Eighteenth-Century Japan," *Journal of Interdisciplinary History*, VI, 3 (Winter 1976), pp. 417–445.

[4] Susan B. Hanley and Kozo Yamamura, "Population Trends and Economic Growth in Pre-industrial Japan," in D. V. Glass and Roger Revelle (eds.), *Population and Social Change* (London, 197.), pp. 485–486.

landownership. The "stagnation" of population growth and the waves of peasant uprisings were seen as evidence of the farmers' hardship. In contrast, we now speak of a rising standard of living and of a land tax rate that was frequently not nearly so oppressive as was once thought, with the majority of farmers engaged in part-time jobs that added much to their income. The easing off in the rate of population growth is attributed less to famine and hardship than to deliberate measures that manifested an increased economic rationality on the part of the peasantry. All of this is not to say that there was not much backbreaking hardship. There was. Conditions varied from region to region—even from valley to valley. There was discontent in the countryside, some of it the result of specific policies of government and some of it of the new class relations in the village.

But if we limit ourselves here to economic developments—increased agricultural productivity, commercialization of the countryside, a relatively low rate of population increase—we have factors that help us explain Japan's rapid industrial development in modern times. Conditions in the villages were preparing the way. Although the political system was heading for trouble, society and the economy ought not to be thought of as declining; rather, we should think of them as growing so strikingly that they could scarcely be held within the bounds of the rigid system established at the outset of the Tokugawa Period.

Growth of the Merchant Class

We have already discussed some of the ways in which the new institutional structure of the Tokugawa system gave rise to a growing commercial economy. We should now consider the emergence of a sizable merchant class in the cities and the difficulties the Tokugawa system found in trying to accommodate it within its structure. This is a development of immense importance for understanding the tensions that were developing within the Tokugawa system by the eighteenth century.

Within the merchant class that grew up there was of course (just as in the other classes) a great deal of disparity. It was not a homogeneous group; rather it ranged from the Osaka financiers at the top, who held the purse strings of many of the daimyo, all the way down to the small shopkeepers, pawnbrokers, journeymen, and peddlers. In between these extremes were wholesalers and shippers who specialized in a variety of commodities and presided over the development of interregional trade. Within local areas there were retailers, brokers, and rural businessmen, some of whom worked in association with han governments to promote commercial development.

The Osaka financiers took advantage of the unique structure of the Tokugawa system to build great merchant houses. They based their strength, in the first place, on the rice-brokering business that was the backbone of Osaka's economy. The major daimyo of central and western Japan, needing cash principally for their alternate attendance requirements, marketed huge amounts of rice in Osaka, and they were dependent on the great merchants of the city to handle all aspects of the transactions. Those merchants began extending to the daimyo long-term loans at high rates of interest. They formed the Osaka banking system in 1670 and eventually dominated the credit system not only of the Osaka area but of all the major trading centers of Japan. Surprisingly sophisticated credit mechanisms and advanced methods of exchange bills developed in order to facilitate trade between these major centers.

Crawcour sums up the influence of these great financiers this way:

Through their exchange and remittance business, they controlled the market in which the relative values of gold and silver—and thus in effect the rate of exchange between Edo and Osaka— were set, and acted as financial agents of the Shogunate. They thus collectively performed some of the functions of a central bank. As commercial and financial agents and major creditors of the various han, they had considerable influence on han economic policy and a practical monopoly of the main exports of the han. Through their handling of tax rice, which amounted to about three-quarters of the supply, they controlled the Osaka rice market and thus the wholesale rice market for the whole country.[5]

Because of the importance they had acquired to the functioning of the Tokugawa system, these financiers were often given quasi-samurai status, sometimes with stipends the equivalent of minor daimyo. Thus although official ideology was often opposed to the growth of the merchant class and commerce in general, in reality government (at all levels) was dependent on merchant groups for their special knowledge in conducting the financial affairs of the system. These groups were often licensed by authorities: given special monopolistic

[5] E. S. Crawcour, "Changes in Japanese Commerce in the Tokugawa Period," in Hall and Jansen (eds.), *Studies in the Institutional History of Early Modern Japan* (Princeton, 1968), p. 196. Copyright © 1968 by Princeton University Press; Princeton Paperback, 1970. Reprinted by permission of Princeton University Press.

privileges in the expectation that they would stabilize prices, assure adequate distribution, and make an annual fee payment.

Urban growth, the spread of a money economy, and the emergence of a vital merchant class were reflected in a vibrant new culture of the townspeople. This development is most closely associated with what is known as the Genroku Period: strictly speaking, only a fifteen-year period from 1688 to 1703, but sometimes designating a fifty-year period stretching roughly from 1680 to 1730, the most brilliant flowering of Japanese culture during the Tokugawa era.

The tenor of this culture was expressed by the term *ukiyo* (meaning "floating world"), which was applied to certain facets of Genroku culture: e.g., *ukiyo-zōshi* ("stories of the floating world") or *ukiyo-e* ("pictures of the floating world"). Originally ukiyo was a Buddhist term referring to the sad impermanence of all earthly things, but during the Genroku Period it shed that religious connotation and came to suggest, rather, a life of pleasure that one accepts without thinking what might lie ahead. One writer in this period defined ukiyo as "living for the moment, gazing at the moon, snow, blossoms, and autumn leaves, enjoying wine, women, and song, and, in general, drifting with the current of life."[6] One might say that both the Buddhists and the townsmen of the Genroku Period agreed that life was fleeting; they simply disagreed as to what one should do about it.

Genroku culture was concentrated primarily in the pleasure quarters, the tea-houses, the theaters, and even the bathhouses of Osaka, Kyoto, and Edo. The castle towns may have shared in Genroku culture, too, but they were certainly far behind. Despite the fact that official ideology put the trading classes at the bottom of the social scale, it was primarily they who were behind this cultural explosion, which included *kabuki*, the puppet theater, the wood block print, and ukiyo literature.

Officials spent their time drawing up lofty Confucian exhortations or devising piecemeal laws in an attempt to control the ostentation, opulence, and extravagance of the trading class and the disruptive influence it was thought to be having on society. Kabuki is a case in point. For almost the whole Tokugawa Period (but especially during Genroku days) there was a running duel between the bakufu and kabuki, the bakufu trying to restrict it and the kabuki always responding with some ingenious evasion. Regarding kabuki as destructive of Con-

---

[6] Howard Hibbett, *The Floating World in Japanese Fiction* (Oxford, 1959), p. 11.

fucian morality, the bakufu banned women from the stage in 1629, and in succeeding years issued regulations designed to segregate kabuki actors from the rest of society and to preserve an austerity of costumes and theater architecture thought to be appropriate for townspeople. Most important was the attempt to eliminate from plays subject matter that might have baneful political influence. Nonetheless some playwrights were able to get away with political satires. For example, one of the most famous playwrights, Chikamatsu Monzaemon (1653–1725), wrote a highly amusing satire of Tokugawa Tsunayoshi (1646–1709), the fifth shogun, who had an idiosyncratic attachment to dogs. Perhaps it was because he had been born in the zodiacal year of the dog. In any case Tsunayoshi was responsible for a stream of legislation protecting the canine family, which earned him the epithet "dog shogun": there were censuses of dogs, dog taxes, dog commissioners and physicians, public kennels, and much else. In a play written in 1714 Chikamatsu seized on Tsunayoshi and his pet projects as splendid objects of satire and by recasting these events in the earlier Kamakura Period was able to evade the censors.

The bakufu's difficulty in coping with the culture of the townsmen was indicative of the much larger problem that officials were having in dealing with the new social and economic conditions that the development of cities and commerce had created. It is useful to think of the Genroku Period as a kind of divide. On the one side, prior to it, the Tokugawa system was becoming established; its political, social, and economic institutions were being systematized. The samurai elite was adjusting to its new role as an administrative bureaucracy and to its new life in the castle towns. Population surged, city life sprang up, land under cultivation was greatly extended, and a new sedentary style of living took hold.

On the other side of the divide, the years after Genroku to which we must now turn our attention, faults were beginning to appear in the political system. "Since the Genroku period," lamented one scholar in the 1730s, ". . . the life of the country has deteriorated."[1] There emerged contradictions between the ideological premises that underlay the system and the reality of the way it was in fact operating. There is always a gap between the ideals of a social system and its actual behavior, but after Genroku the gap in Japan was too wide to be overlooked. Behind the facade of political stability, immense social and economic developments occurred that gradually transformed the system. In many different areas these developments created strains. Let us examine them rather arbitrarily under the headings of economic, social, and ideological problems.

Economic Problems

The fundamental problem creating strains within the Tokugawa political system was

CRISIS IN THE TOKUGAWA SYSTEM

[1] Quoted in Tetsuo Najita, "Political Economism in the Thought of Dazai Shundai (1680–1747)," *Journal of Asian Studies*, XXXI, 4 (August 1972), p. 836.

the transformation of its economic basis and consequent undermining of the premises upon which the system had been founded. The soaring expenditures of the bakufu and of the individual daimyo tended more and more to exceed their income, which was largely drawn from the land tax levied on the peasants. Expenditures of the lord grew continuously, partly because, with the urban growth, government became more complex. Then, too, it was sometimes less efficient. Laxity and corruption were not uncommon. Social functions associated with government became increasingly elaborate and expensive, and gift giving grew to immense proportions.

The alternate attendance system continued enormously expensive for the daimyo. By the latter part of the Tokugawa Period, the typical lord was devoting as much as 70 to 80 percent of his normal expenditures to costs connected with the system. In addition, not infrequently there were emergency or extraordinary outlays to rebuild mansions after fires, to entertain the shogun, or to cover the costs of marriages, funerals, and other ceremonies in Edo. The steady stream of sumptuary laws, which sought to restrict ostentation in food and dress, indicate that extravagance and conspicuous consumption were a way of life among the upper classes.

Government frequently was unable to generate the added revenues necessary to defray its soaring expenses. Some daimyo succeeded in developing additional sources of income, principally through development of new cash crops that were run as han monopolies, but for the most part they continued to be largely dependent on the land tax and on rice production, which accounted for a shrinking portion of the total economy. Daimyo were often at a disadvantage when they converted their rice income into money at Osaka. There, they were at the mercy of the astute merchant financiers and the vagaries of the rice market. It was possible, of course, that a good harvest, together with capable and honest administration, could increase the coffers of the shogun or the daimyo. In general, however, much more frequently revenues fell short because of bad luck or bad management, and expenditures rose because of extravagance, corruption, and the increased complexity of government.

A negative reason for the financial troubles of government was the overall failure to develop adequate methods for taxing the growing sectors of the economy. For example, during the Tokugawa Period there was a great increase in agricultural productivity, which should have allowed the lord to increase the land tax. Yet research seems to indicate that land, from about 1700 on, ceased to be surveyed periodically and thus there was often no adequate accounting of increased productivity. Toward the end of the Tokugawa Period, therefore, in some areas taxes were based on assessments that were a century or more out of date. It is difficult to say why land surveys were neglected, but undoubtedly bureaucratic inertia and consideration of the massive administrative effort required to survey an entire domain were partly responsible. Still another factor may have been fear of resistance from the peasants. Whatever the reasons, growing wealth in the agricultural sector was generally not taxed in any systematic way.

Nor was commerce, the most rapidly expanding part of the economy, taxed in a uniform, consistent manner. There were piecemeal attempts, but perhaps the lack of bookkeeping methods and of bureaucratic determination deterred government from more systematic means. Instead it relied, for example, on granting monopolistic privileges to merchant guilds in return for fees. Another type of commercial taxation, if it can properly be called such, was the exaction from wealthy merchants and farmers of forced "loans," which were generally not repaid. In the latter part of the period both the bakufu and the domains had frequent recourse to this method of raising revenues.

Social Problems

As a result of the increasing economic troubles in which government found itself, it was frequently unable to meet its most important financial commitment: the paying of warrior stipends. Often the lord solved his financial problems by passing them on to his retainers. By the end of the eighteenth century it was common to cut warrior stipends, sometimes by as much as 50 percent.

Such a solution may have temporarily eased the daimyo's economic problems, but it only added to increasing unrest in the society he had to govern. By the end of the Tokugawa Period, as a result of their diminished income, perhaps the majority of samurai lived in honorable but austere circumstances. Of course there was considerable variation in samurai income between domains. For instance, a Tosa samurai traveling to Satsuma in late Tokugawa discovered that stipends considered low in his native Tosa would seem generous in Satsuma. It is clear, however, that nearly everywhere the number of "upper" samurai, living in comfortable circumstances, was small compared to the mass of samurai who lived in straitened circumstances. The well-being of the upper strata of the peasant and merchant class was often superior to that of the ordinary samurai. And this anomaly put a great strain on warrior loyalty; it was humiliating and contributed to deteriorating morale.

Like the daimyo and the bakufu, the samurai had to take steps to alleviate his financial difficulty. Many of his measures were makeshift and often they were degrading, sorely wounding warrior pride. Hard-pressed for money, some samurai adopted merchant boys into their family or married their children to the children of their merchant creditors. Another recourse was to pawn the family armor. Poorer samurai practiced infanticide to reduce their economic liabilities. A large number of the poorer samurai families eked out their inadequate stipends through cottage industries, such as the making of straw sandals. Occasionally, by the nineteenth century, some impoverished samurai simply abandoned their feudal duties, giving up their diminished stipends in return for a better living as commoners.

We ought not to think of the samurai as uniformly mired in poverty. Not only was there a great deal of differentiation within the class as a whole and considerable regional variation, it is also true that much of what is referred to as the increasing "poverty" of the samurai was relative. In the case of some members of the warrior class whose income remained stable, their discontent sprang from unfulfilled wants, rising expectations, and a feeling of being deprived of the fruits of a growing economy. In other words, for such warriors there was an element of psychological poverty involved: they felt themselves deprived because they were unable to buy commodities that members of other classes could afford.

We find a perfect example of growing prosperity among commoners in the upper levels of the farming class. The gōnō (wealthy peasants) were an anomalous group within the Tokugawa class structure. Officially, of course, they were peasants and lived in the village, but by the late Tokugawa Period they were set off from other commoners by their wealth and power in the countryside. Not only were they often village headmen and large holders of land, but they were also engaged in a variety of rural commercial enterprises, such as money lending, sake brewing, dyeing, or silk and cotton weaving. Their investments in land and rural industries enabled them to support a lifestyle quite in contrast to their official status. Through contributions to their daimyo's treasury many gained the right to wear swords, bear surnames, and send their sons to the domain academy—all privileges ordinarily reserved for the warrior. The social distance between this group and the samurai was thus rapidly narrowing, and the feelings of many aggrieved warriors at such signs of institutional disintegration and moral decay were summed up by one angry contemporary:

Now the most lamentable abuse of the present day among the peasants is that those who have become wealthy forget their status and live luxuriously like city aristocrats. . . . They build [homes] with the most handsome and wonderful gates, porches, beams, alcoves, ornamental shelves, and libraries. . . . They themselves wear fine clothes and imitate the ceremonial style of warriors on all such occasions as weddings, celebrations, and masses for the dead.[2]

Class relations were becoming diffuse and difficult to accommodate within the rigid class structure established at the outset of the Tokugawa Period. The spactacle of growing wealth within the commoner classes was doubtless evidence to warriors of institutional disintegration and of moral decay. Respect for rank and the traditional virtues of frugality, industry, and modesty seemed jeopardized. On the other hand, in the biographies of able and wealthy commoners at the end of the Tokugawa Period, there is plenty of resentment and frustration over the fact that the Tokugawa system set strict limits on their social advancement. One finds this particularly among the wealthy peasants.

Of course not all peasants were so fortunate as the gōnō. Like the other classes, there was great disparity of wealth: large numbers of the peasantry lived at the subsistence level, terribly at the mercy of the vicissitudes of the weather and the market. Famines on a nationwide scale occurred in the 1720s, the 1780s, and the 1830s as a result of unseasonable weather, and not coincidentally waves of peasant uprisings occurred during the 1780s and the 1830s. Such outbreaks were usually directed against the wealthy, the moneylenders, and local officials. These riots were the ultimate protest that peasants could make against unbearable conditions, and though they were often not political in intent they held political meaning, for this form of protest was a specter that any lord might fear in pondering the possibility of increasing the land tax. Nor were the uprisings simply blind outbursts. Often they had very specific goals, such as the remission of certain taxes, the removal of a particular official, or the correction of some local abuse.

The peasant disturbances of the 1830s culminated in a series of incidents that followed an abortive uprising in Osaka in 1837 led by Ōshio Heihachirō. Ōshio was a minor bakufu official who accused his superiors of callous disregard for the

---

[2] Quoted in Thomas C. Smith, *Political Change and Industrial Development in Japan: Government Enterprise, 1868–1880* (Stanford, 1955), pp. 17–18.

suffering of common people and plotted an uprising that he hoped would spark other attacks against the established order. Although fires raged for two days through the merchant section of the city, the rebellion was easily quelled by bakufu forces. News of the uprising, however, encouraged others in surrounding provinces.

Such indications of social strain and discontent have led many historians to write of the "decay of feudalism" and to stress in their descriptions the breakdown of the Tokugawa system. This is of course valid. But one should also stress growth—a society growing and changing so markedly that it could no longer be contained within the institutional bounds established by Tokugawa Ieyasu at the beginning of the period.

Ideological Problems

Social discontent within the samurai class was exacerbated by ideological problems that grew out of conflict between the theory and practice of the Tokugawa system. One such problem concerned the appointment of officials in the bakufu and han bureaucracies, which according to widely held principles should have been based on merit. In actual practice, however, after the early Tokugawa Period appointments were made mainly on the basis of social rank. With occasional exceptions the most important offices went to the higher-ranking samurai, and frustration over this situation among young, lower-ranking warriors became one of the greatest forces for change by the beginning of the nineteenth century. The historian Sir George Sansom, in fact, wrote that among all the causes of the anti-Tokugawa movement that led to the downfall of the bakufu, the most powerful was the ambition of young samurai. As the status system gradually hardened, official appointment came to be determined largely by hereditary succession and social rank. By the end of Genroku, the vested interests were entrenched.

Among able, lively, lower-ranking young samurai there grew a restless dissatisfaction with the rigidity of the system. They felt unjustly cut off from positions of power and respect; they favored more freedom of movement within the hierarchy; and they opposed hereditary restraints upon such mobility. Many writers who urged that the appointment and promotion of officials be based upon merit alone argued that because of environmental factors ability was to be found especially among lower warriors. They said that hardship and adversity made for intelligence and character, while the wealth and ease of upper-level warriors made for foolishness and corruption. Blaming the hereditary principle for the failures of government, they sometimes wrote thinly veiled attacks upon the daimyo, who, they implied, were pompous and weak. Despite the implications of these writings, they were not intended as a revolutionary attack on the system. The discontented young warriors were dissatisfied not so much with the system of social hierarchy itself as with their own position in it.

The educational system was partly responsible for the surfacing of this problem, for it tended to call attention to ability. With the spread of domain schools from the middle of Tokugawa on, it became harder to conceal the wide discrepancies between talent demonstrated in the classroom and official appointment based upon hereditary rank.

Other aspects of Tokugawa ideology also manifested contradictions between theory and practice. Loyalty, for example, was the basic virtue upon which samurai training and discipline were organized, but the conditions upon which this key value was based had been utterly transformed during the course of the Tokugawa Period. A profound change in the nature of loyalty and in the relationship between vassal and lord had taken place. During the Warring States Period and the early years of Tokugawa rule, loyalty had two important characteristics:

1. *Loyalty was conditional.* It was based on a bilateral relationship between the lord and his vassal; the lord absolutely depended upon the loyalty of his samurai followers in order to maintain his position and his territory. Without it, his fief would quickly be lost to a neighboring lord. On the other hand, the vassals received in return for their allegiance a fief or a stipend. The relationship was, therefore, vital and mutually dependent, and it was conditional upon both sides fulfilling their functions. When a lord gave signs of weakness, it was not uncommon for vassals to desert him and join a neighboring lord who might better protect and reward them. There were many cases of treachery, of vassals overthrowing their lord. Loyalty was therefore a real, live value—to observe or renounce.

2. *Loyalty was also personal.* Since power was private, there was no higher authority (neither government nor law) that could enforce the relationship. "The lord," writes Albert Craig, "had no court of appeal beyond his own strength should a vassal be disloyal."[3] Loyalty in the Warring States Period was often, Thomas Smith adds, "an intimate, intensely emotional relationship, based in no small part on the personal qualities of

---

[3] Craig, *Chōshū in the Meiji Restoration* (Cambridge, Mass., 1961), p. 145.

the lord, a relationship which existed between men who had fought side by side, grieved together at the loss of comrades, whose safety and families' safety depended on their keeping the faith."[4]

During the Tokugawa Period the lord-vassal relation underwent a silent but profound change:

1. *Loyalty became unconditional.* It was now based on a unilateral relationship; it lost its mutual dependency. With warfare ended, the lord no longer needed to worry about the loyalty of his vassals, for his position was guaranteed by the shogunate and it was virtually impossible for the vassals to leave or overthrow him. The loyalty of the vassal, in other words, was no longer conditional upon the lord's effectiveness as a leader, upon his ability to compensate and protect his retainers. The samurai, under the Tokugawa system, could do no other than give unquestioning obedience to his daimyo—even if his stipend were sharply reduced by his financially troubled lord (a measure no lord would have dared resort to in the Warring States era).

2. *Loyalty became impersonal.* The relationship between lord and vassal became distant and formal, drained of much of its emotional content by the new circumstances. No longer their leader in war, the lord had less contact with his retainers. Owing to the alternate attendance system, many daimyo were born and raised in Edo and spent a great part of their mature life there. For long periods out of personal touch with conditions in the home fief, such a lord came to be looked on as an administrative head, sometimes little more than a titular leader.

Since their position was hereditary under the Tokugawa and no longer depended on their personal abilities, the lords often lacked qualities of leadership. The inability of government to deal with domestic and external problems called attention to this problem, and the daimyo came in for increasing criticism by the beginning of the nineteenth century. The daimyo, one contemporary writer observed scornfully, "were brought up by women, where no sound of the outside world penetrated and not even officials or retainers dared enter; therefore they knew nothing of men and affairs. Whatever nonsense they spoke was praised as wisdom, every action treated as a miracle of grace and dexterity. If they played chess or any other game, their companions contrived that they won, then threw up their hands, exclaiming 'My, how clever the lord is!' "[5] Although not typical,

---

[4] Thomas C. Smith, "Japan's Aristocratic Revolution," *Yale Review*, L, 3 (1961), p. 376. Copyright © Yale University.

[5] Thomas C. Smith, " 'Merit' as Ideology in the Tokugawa Period," in R. P. Dore (ed.), *Aspects of Social Change in Modern Japan* (Princeton, 1967), p. 86.

criticism of the daimyo as weak, foolish, self-indulgent, or incompetent was expressed with increased frequency as the crisis in the Tokugawa system deepened.

In these circumstances one can discern among warriors a longing for a more satisfying form of loyalty. For however much it was bereft of its former emotional significance, loyalty was still a primary value. Every samurai boy internalized it as he grew up. Yet it was scarcely fulfilling to give loyalty to one whose abilities and character were less than peerless or who appeared to be a distant unconcerned leader. In fact what seems to have occurred was that loyalty as a value remained strong but, as the lord became a more remote figure, it was directed more and more towards the han itself—a kind of "han nationalism," as Craig has called it. Or, to put it another way, loyalty was now given to the lord less because he was an admired individual leader than because he was a symbol of the han.

This transformation in the nature of loyalty helped to prepare the way for modern nationalism. Since loyalty was no longer closely tied to an individual but was rather directed toward the governmental unit with which warriors identified (i.e., their han), when Commodore Matthew Perry arrived and created the foreign crisis that threatened the nation, consciousness of belonging to Japan was heightened. Loyalty was rather quickly shifted from the han to the nation. There were, in fact, signs of growing national consciousness everywhere on the literary scene in the late Tokugawa Period. An awakened interest in the national tradition was apparent in the curriculum of many domain schools, which encouraged knowledge of Japan's past as a useful addition to Confucian studies. Outside of official education the growth of the *kokugaku* (national studies) movement was more strident, exhorting pride in the unique and superior qualities of Japanese culture.

Movements for Reform in Government

In order to deal with the mounting difficulties of government, reform movements were initiated within the shogunate and many of the domains. It is exceedingly difficult to generalize about these movements because the measures taken and the success achieved varied greatly.

Generally, however, we may distinguish two main strands of reformist thinking. The first and dominant one was what we may call the "fundamentalist" approach, whose main purpose was to restore the fundamental or "purer" conditions of the early Tokugawa Period. Idealizing a purely agrarian economy, this approach sought in various ways to suppress or at least restrain the growing power of the merchant class. It stressed retrenchment in government and revival of the moral values of simplicity, austerity, and frugality. It was characterized by heavy reliance on sumptuary edicts, seeking to limit and curtail consumption. Only occasionally did this approach try to increase the income of government, and when it did it tended to be through a time-honored method, such as land reclamation. Some of the more extreme proponents of the fundamentalist school urged return of the samurai to the countryside, relocating them in the villages where they would be away from the corrupting influences of the towns. It was expected not only that the morale of the samurai would thereby be raised, but that the function of the castle town merchants would likewise be weakened.

The other approach to reform may be called the "realist" school because it accepted the growing commercialization of the economy and urged the authorities to adjust to it, not deny it. The realists agreed that the warrior class could not continue to stand aloof from and disdain financial matters. They urged a reorientation in Tokugawa thinking, a recognition that trade could be productive and that government could profit from the commercial segments of the economy. The realist school urged government to encourage the production of capital wealth and to use its political power to set up state enterprises and monopoly organizations. Some of its more extreme proponents urged abandonment of the seclusion policy and revival of foreign trade as a means of bringing wealth to Japan. The latter argument aroused bitter opposition, but the proposals for state-sponsored trade and industry were accepted to an increasing degree by the shogunate and many domain governments.

Some of the reform attempts by the bakufu and the han bureaucracies were a mixture of these two approaches, but most leaned toward fundamentalism and achieved only limited success. The bakufu had made several efforts at reform, but the wave of peasant uprisings in the 1830s and Ōshio's spectacular rebellion in Osaka in 1837, which set fires raging through the merchant quarters and brought bakufu troops to subdue the rebels, gave notice that the problems of government were far from solved.

The final effort of the shogunate to deal with these problems, prior to the intervention of the foreigners, came in the reforms of the early 1840s. The leading figure of the bakufu in this period was Mizuno Tadakuni, who rose in 1841 to leadership in the Council of Elders, the shogunate's controlling administrative organ, and took charge of this last concerted reform program. His reforms leaned toward the fundamentalist approach, relying heavily on sumptuary legislation and, in addition, attempting to disband merchant associations and to stem the flow of immigrants into Edo from the countryside. Such traditionalistic reforms failed, for they treated the symptoms rather than the root causes of bakufu distress.

Japan's economy and society were far too changed and too dynamic to be pressed back into the mold of early Tokugawa institutions. The failure of Mizuno's reform program gave added support to the contention of realist reform thinkers that a comprehensive change in the political structure of the country was necessary, so that institutions might be adjusted to the changed conditions of the society and economy.

At this point, while the bakufu and many domains were still struggling with their unresolved problems, the foreign crisis developed and very suddenly brought matters to a head. We may think of it as a catalyst, speeding up the reaction to pressing domestic problems that otherwise might have been allowed to continue unresolved for some time longer.

The foreign crisis quickly galvanized the forces for change. The remarkable responsiveness of Japanese society to the Western challenge is thus, in part, to be understood as resulting from the gradual buildup of social and economic problems during the preceding century. Had Japan not been characterized at this time by institutional incapacity, widespread social unrest, and an anxious groping by political leaders for new reform measures, the Japanese response would doubtless have been more ponderous and reluctant.

The Coming of the Foreign Crisis

In contrast to domestic problems, which had been developing since the Genroku Period, the foreign intervention occurred abruptly, with a suddenness and intensity surely unexpected by most politically conscious Japanese. There had been forewarnings—occasional omens—as early as the 1790s that the time-honored exclusion policy was in jeopardy, but they were infrequent and easily forgotten in the press of more immediate concerns.

Russia had posed the initial problems. Its envoys and traders began appearing on the islands north of Hokkaido in the 1790s, seeking to open trade relations with Japan. In every case they were rebuffed, and after 1813 there was no further contact for several decades. In the meantime, however, the British, having extended their power into

THE MEIJI RESTORATION

5

India and Malaysia, had begun to build up a China trade and to probe Japanese coastal waters. A series of incidents ensued, beginning in 1808 when a British frigate flouted the exclusion decrees by sailing into Nagasaki harbor demanding supplies of food and water. It was not, however, until word was received of the Opium War (1839–1842) in China, which ended in British acquisition of Hong Kong and the forced opening of five ports to British trade and residence, that concern spread in Japan that a serious challenge to the seclusion policy was imminent. To the Japanese who thought about it, expanding British power in the Far East represented a distinct threat. The Dutch, in fact, acting through their trading station representatives in Nagasaki, warned the bakufu in 1844 of the situation and urged that the country be opened voluntarily before Western nations undertook to force Japan to this decision.

As it transpired, while Britain was preoccupied with its new involvement in China, the United States took the lead in forcefully testing the "closed door policy." The opening of Chinese treaty ports presaged a new era of national rivalry among the Western powers in the Far East, with America too acquiring trading interests on the China coast. Taken together with the settlement of the disputed claims to the Oregon Territory in 1846 and the acquisition of California in 1848, these interests gave the American government cause for much greater attention to Pacific affairs. In 1852 President Millard Fillmore approved the mission that would be headed by Commodore Matthew C. Perry to try to establish relations with the Japanese government. The Perry mission originated in the desire to protect shipwrecked American sailors and to acquire coaling stations and the right for ships to take on provisions. But deeper than those reasons lay the hope for trade and the conviction that America had a destiny to expand its interests in the Pacific.

Although apprised by the Dutch of the mission well in advance, the bakufu was nonetheless uncertain how to deal with it. When Perry arrived with his squadron of four ships and anchored off the coast on July 8, 1853, political opinion in Edo was confused and divided. Almost all of those who thought about the problem were agreed on the need for strengthening defenses to meet the threat of foreign attack. On other questions of foreign policy, thought was sharply divided between the kaikoku (open country) school and the jōi (expel the barbarian) school.

The kaikoku school was closely associated with and drew its strength from a small number of Japanese, known as "Dutch scholars," who were familiar with Western technology and science. As early as 1720, the seclusion edicts had been eased to the extent of allowing Western books to circulate in Japan so long as they did not expound Christian doctrine. This decision was made by Tokugawa Yoshimune, a shogun who had a serious interest in the Western calendar as well as curiosity about astronomy, watchmaking, geography, and other topics he encountered from the agents of the Dutch trading station who visited Edo. By the middle of the eighteenth century some translation work was beginning, and "Dutch studies" gained added importance as the efficacy of Western medicine began to be demonstrated. By the eve of Perry's arrival, as a result of the small but growing number of Dutch scholars, the Japanese had a considerable store of knowledge of the West and of its technology. There were translations of Western treatises on astronomy, chemistry, geography, mathematics, physics, and (as attention turned to problems of defense) on ballistics, metallurgy, and military tactics. Many scholars have argued that already, at that time, knowledge of Western science was more widespread in Japan than in any other Asian country. Keenly aware of the West's more advanced technology and of Japan's military weakness, the Dutch scholars argued pragmatically that in the changed conditions of the nineteenth century the policy of national seclusion was no longer effective. They believed that Japan needed Western weapons and techniques in order to defend it; therefore it must avoid war with a Western power at least until it had a chance to strengthen itself—even if that meant giving in to foreign demands for the opening of ports.

Those who favored opening the country were generally of what we have called the realist school of reform thought, regarding foreign trade as an opportunity for bakufu profit and therefore as contributing directly to the solution of the financial problems of government. There was of course a good deal of variation among those who advocated an open country, but most of them saw it primarily as a matter of national defense. They saw an open country not necessarily as good in itself but rather as a means to create a strong and independent Japan.

One of the leaders of this kind of argument was Sakuma Shōzan (1811–1864), a samurai-scholar who exercised considerable influence, partly through his followers and partly through his lord, who was a bakufu councillor. As a young man he studied Western gunnery, and then, turning to other aspects of Dutch studies, became convinced of the critical importance of such technology to his country's defense. In particular, his thinking was influential for its insistence on the application of pragmatic ideas rather than abstract moral principles. Thus he referred again and again to his belief that "Eastern ethics and Western science" were both proper in their separate spheres. Confucian morals remained valid as a criterion for personal behavior, but it was necessary for political leaders to look beyond Confucian scholarship for answers to the practical problems of governance. Impressed by the example of Peter the Great, he proposed the appointment of "men of talent in military strategy, planning, and administration" to carry out a program of national strengthening by establishing relations with foreign countries, obtaining the advantages of foreign technology, and building up defense through a new political structure.

Sakuma was assassinated in 1864. His views had been violently opposed by jōi (expel the barbarian) samurai, who passionately believed that opening the country would bring political and cultural disaster. To them China's defeat in the Opium War was attributable less to Western military techniques than to the contamination of Chinese society by Western customs and religion. Jōi thinking was often pervaded by an intense xenophobia and cultural chauvinism. Aizawa Seishisai, whose essays inspired the jōi school, wrote, for example, of Japan's place in the world:

The earth in the firmament appears to be perfectly round, without edges or corners. However, everything exists in its natural bodily form, and our Divine Land is situated at the top of the earth. Thus, although it is not an extensive country spatially, it reigns over all quarters of the world, for it has never once changed its dynasty or its form of sovereignty. The various countries of the West correspond to the feet and legs of the body. That is why their ships come from afar to visit Japan. As for the land amidst the seas which the Western barbarians call America, it occupies the hindmost region of the earth; thus its people are stupid and simple, and are incapable of doing things.[1]

A more reasoned defense of jōi was offered by Confucianists, who thought that Western religion would undermine the ethical basis of Japanese society and who believed that Western trade, bringing greater wealth to merchants, would in turn be destructive of morals. They did not accept Sakuma Shōzan's pragmatic advocacy of preserving traditional ethical values while adopting the new technology. "To say that we can accept Western science although we must reject Western moral teaching as evil and wrong," wrote the conservative Ōhashi Totsuan,

[1] Ryusaku Tsunoda *et al.* (eds.), *Sources of Japanese Tradition* (New York, 1958), p. 596.

"is like telling people that although the mainstream of a river is poisoned yet they can safely drink from the sidestreams."[2] In a sense, he and like-minded Confucianists were right. The threat was cultural, for it would be impossible (as was subsequently demonstrated) to preserve traditional values unchanged, once Western science was accepted.

In their moral conservatism the jōi advocates had much in common with the fundamentalist school of domestic reform. They saw positive benefit in armed resistance to the Westerners, for they expected hostilities to revive samurai morale and to restore habits of discipline and frugality. Furthermore, they regarded foreign trade as harmful, bringing a loss of specie and further disruption of the economy.

The Treaties

Perry presented his demands for treaty relations in the summer of 1853 and then withdrew, warning that he would return the following spring for an answer. Abe Masahirō, the head of the bakufu's Council of Elders and the effective head of government owing to the incompetence of the shogun, temporized. Faced with sharp divisions of opinion, aware that antiforeign feeling was strong but believing that Western demands could not long be resisted, he sought to gain consensus by requesting all the daimyo to express their opinions regarding American demands. This unprecedented step amounted to a confession of the bakufu's weakness, nor did the daimyo's responses produce the basis for concerted action vis-à-vis the foreign powers.

Within bakufu circles, during the winter of 1853–54, policy was debated. The most powerful of the hereditary (fudai) lords, Ii Naosuke, expressed what soon became the dominant view in the bakufu when he advocated a positive, kaikoku response, adding: "When one is besieged in a castle, to raise the drawbridge is to imprison oneself and make it impossible to hold out indefinitely."[3] He therefore urged a period of trade that would allow Japan to acquire the knowledge necessary to defend her independence.

When Perry returned, this time with a flotilla of eight ships,

2 Carmen Blacker, "Ōhashi Totsuan: A Study in Anti-Western Thought," in Transactions of the Asiatic Society of Japan, series 3, vol. 7 (Tokyo, 1959), p. 165.
3 W. G. Beasley, Select Documents on Japanese Foreign Policy, 1853–1868 (London, 1955), p. 117.

Commodore Perry arrives to meet with the Japanese. *National Archives*

the bakufu acceded to his demands. A treaty was signed on March 31, 1854 (the so-called Kanagawa Treaty of Friendship), which provided that two ports, Shimoda and Hakodate, would be opened to American ships and limited trade, and that an American consular agent was to be permitted to reside in Shimoda. Prior to the signing of the treaty there was a ceremony at which the Americans presented several tokens of their civilization as gifts, including a model railroad, a telegraph set, farm tools, and a hundred gallons of whiskey. The Japanese, for their part, put on a demonstration of *sumō* wrestling, and the Americans then responded with a minstrel show. Afterwards Perry, who had something of the self-confident and pompous air of another American military figure who arrived in Japan almost a century later, concluded that "Japan had been opened to the nations of the West" and that "the Japanese are, undoubtedly, like the Chinese, a very imitative, adaptive, and compliant people and in these characteristics may be discovered a promise of the comparatively easy introduction of foreign customs and habits, if not of the nobler principles and better life of a higher civilization."[4]

[4] W. G. Beasley, *The Meiji Restoration* (Stanford, 1972), p. 96.

Shortly after the signing of the Treaty of Kanagawa, the bakufu concluded similar treaties with Britain, Russia, and Holland. The shogunate took solace from having forestalled any large-scale opening to trade, but this comfort proved short-lived for, unsatisfied with anything less than full commercial treaties, the Western powers in succeeding years put increased pressure on the shogunate to grant still further concessions. Again, it was an American, Townsend Harris, who played the leading role. Harris came to Shimoda in 1856 as the first American consul. He set about at once to persuade the authorities that further opening to trade was inevitable and that it would be far better to conclude a reasonable agreement with his country than to await the forceful demands of other powers. As evidence, he pointed to the outbreak of the Anglo-French War in 1856 and to the likelihood that the British fleet assembled for the war against China would next be used to extract a commercial treaty from the Japanese. Harris's tact and persistence paid off. Hotta Masayoshi, who had succeeded Abe Masahirō as the senior member of the bakufu's Council of Elders, was convinced of the irresistibility of foreign demands as well as the positive benefit of foreign intercourse for the building of Japanese defenses. "Our policy," he concluded, "should be to stake everything on the present opportunity, to conclude friendly alliances, to send ships to foreign countries everywhere and conduct trade, to copy the foreigners where they are at their best and so repair our own shortcomings, to foster our national strength and complete our armaments, and so gradually subject the foreigners to our influence until in the end all the countries of the world know the blessings of perfect tranquillity and our hegemony is acknowledged throughout the globe."[5]

On July 29, 1858 the Harris Treaty was signed. It became the model for similar treaties signed in the following weeks with Britain, France, Holland, and Russia. They provided essentially three things: (1) Edo, Kobe, Nagasaki, Niigata, and Yokohama were opened to foreign trade; (2) Japanese tariffs were placed under international control and import duties were fixed at low levels; and (3) a system of extraterritoriality was established, which provided that foreign residents would be subject to their own consular courts rather than to Japanese law.

These unequal treaties imposed for the first time in Japan's history extensive restrictions on its national sovereignty, and, while they did not require the cession of any territory (such as the powers required elsewhere in Asia), they placed Japan in a

---

[5] *Ibid.*, p. 117.

semicolonial status. In the long run the treaties became a symbol of the national impotence that was exposed by renewed contact with the West, and recovery of national independence and international respect became an overriding goal, which the Japanese pursued with extraordinary tenacity. In the short run the treaties ignited political conflict that destroyed bakufu authority and led, a decade later, to the establishment of a new government.

Declining Fortunes of the Bakufu

By breaking with the 250-year tradition of the Tokugawa government and referring Perry's demands to all the lords for their frank opinion, the shogunate unwittingly encouraged open debate and criticism of all its policies. In this situation it became increasingly difficult to stop the unraveling of bakufu authority. In 1858 Hotta Masayoshi, the effective head of government, sought the approval of the imperial court to the draft of the Harris Treaty—tantamount to still further confession of weakness. He hoped thereby to defuse what he knew would be bitter opposition to the treaty, but he also revealed the declining authority of the bakufu, and, when the court refused, this was clear for all to see. Rebuffed by the newly emboldened Emperor and nobles, Hotta was forced to resign.

Under his replacement, Ii Naosuke, the strongest of the fudai lords, there was a brief resurgence of bakufu strength. Ii took forceful steps to assert his authority. Disregarding the attitude of the imperial court, he ordered the signing of the Harris Treaty and afterward compelled the court to give its consent. Then he ordered into retirement or house arrest all the daimyo who had opposed his policies. These strong-arm methods, however, further inflamed the bitterness that many fanatical samurai felt toward the bakufu for having conceded so much to the barbarians. On a snowy day in March 1860, as his procession was entering the gate of the shogun's castle, Ii was assassinated.

It was a decisive event. Ii's successors proved less able and less forceful than he; the full tide of anti-bakufu sentiment, which had been gathering since 1854, now swept over them. They were unable to control the flow of events that carried the bakufu toward its demise. After the assassination, opponents of the shogunate and its policies looked to the imperial court as a counterweight. The daimyo of Satsuma proposed a "union of court and bakufu" so as to improve the position of the court. The shogunate accepted the proposal, hoping to use the court's prestige to shore up its own, but to gain court backing it was forced to make several damaging concessions. The bakufu was compelled to appoint to high positions in the shogunate reform-minded officials who were to implement the "union." Under the influence of these officials, the bakufu approved a relaxation of its control measures, permitting family hostages to leave Edo and diminishing the alternate attendance requirement to a mere one hundred days every three years. Symbolically, the most important concession was the agreement of the shogun that he would travel to Kyoto to consult with the court on national policies, thereby rendering himself to some extent accountable to the Emperor. When Tokugawa Iemochi made the trip in the spring of 1863, even his extraordinary procession of three thousand retainers could not conceal the momentous fact that it was the first time since the seventeenth century that a shogun had felt compelled to visit Kyoto.

In the aftermath of these concessions, the bakufu found it difficult to exercise its will over the most powerful daimyo. The domain of Chōshū tried to carry out an antiforeigner policy by firing on foreign vessels passing through the Strait of Shimonoseki, adjacent to the domain. When, under pressure from the powers, the bakufu sent an emissary to Chōshū ordering that it desist, extremist samurai in the domain killed him as he fled after delivering the message. Shortly thereafter forces from Chōshū marched on Kyoto and attempted to stage a coup and establish its influence in the imperial court.

The attempt failed, but the shogunate decided to organize a punitive expedition to punish Chōshū's overt disobedience and its breaking of the Tokugawa peace. A force of 150,000 samurai, drawn from the chief domains, was assembled on the borders of Chōshū in late 1864, but the participation of many of the domains was half-hearted and the bakufu therefore could not plan a sustained campaign. Instead, through the mediation of Saigō Takamori of Satsuma, a lenient settlement was agreed upon, requiring a formal apology and the suicide of three senior officials held to be responsible for the attempted coup in Kyoto.

Despite the qualified character of its success, the bakufu took heart from this assertion of its leadership. It tried to achieve total restoration of its authority by reimposing the alternate attendance system, by sending troops to Kyoto to establish control over the court, and by acquiring French technical assistance in building up its military strength. The specter of a bakufu attempt to re-establish its former supremacy alienated many lords and brought the two most powerful domains, Chōshū and Satsuma, together in a secret alliance to work for the restoration of imperial rule. The alliance became operative in 1866 when the shogunate, confronted with renewed defiance from Chōshū, organized a second punitive expedition. This time several of the major domains, including Satsuma, refused to participate; Chōshū, using modern weapons and buoyed by superior morale, roundly defeated the bakufu forces, who sued for peace and withdrew.

Samurai Activists

In the last chapter we discussed the deep discontent among able lower-ranking warriors, who felt unjustly cut off from higher office by the rigidities of the hereditary system. This latent discontent came to the surface in many of the prominent domains after Perry's arrival, for the treaties raised fierce emotions and opened up political issues to much wider discussion. Moreover, they created a sense of crisis in which the argument for promoting men of talent took on new force, and the effectiveness of the traditional ruling segment of the samurai was more insistently called into question.

Not only were the new activists of lower rank, they were young—representatives of a generation that was to provide Japan with new leadership in the aftermath of the Meiji Restoration. Because of their temperament, their involvement in plots and conspiracies, and their resort to violence and assassination, many were known as *shishi*, "men of spirit." They were a wenching, impulsive, devil-may-care type of young man, passionately devoted to the imperial cause, which they called the highest loyalty of all. "The shishi had no care for the morrow. He was brave, casual, carefree, took himself very seriously where 'first things' were concerned, and was utterly indifferent where they were not. Irresponsible in many matters, he was also a roisterer, given to wine and women."[6] Flouting conventional standards of morality and feudal discipline, the shishi were symptomatic of a search for a more satisfying loyalty and for a new political and social order.

Lacking a clear revolutionary program, they reacted to Perry's coming with a burst of emotion that was initially di-

---

[6] Marius B. Jansen, *Sakamoto Ryōma and the Meiji Restoration* (Princeton, 1961), p. 98.

rected at the barbarian. Only after the bakufu acquiesced in the Harris Treaty did they vent their fury on the shogunate and others of the ruling elite, whom they held personally responsible for the plight of Japan. Ii Naosuke and many other officials were assassinated by shishi angered at their failure to expel the foreigner.

Yoshida Shoin (1830–1859) is one of the best remembered of these activists for the influence he had on Chōshū samurai. He studied under Sakuma Shōzan in Edo, became convinced of the need for Western learning for the defense of Japan, and attempted to leave Japan with Perry's squadron to continue his studies in America. He was apprehended by bakufu officials and returned to Chōshū, where he opened a school and gathered about him a group of shishi passionately committed to the imperial institution and to national defense. Among his group of students were future leaders of modern Japan, including Yamagata Aritomo and Itō Hirobumi. The signing of the Harris Treaty of 1858 aroused them, as it did shishi all over the country, to violent action. The fury that had previously been directed at the barbarians was now turned on the bakufu. In many domains young samurai of all ranks became involved in politics, and fanatical activity by shishi sought the removal of "evil" officials who stood in the way of radical opposition to the foreigners.

The shishi, however, were soon given convincing demonstrations of the irresistibility of Western military power, which served to calm their fanaticism and redirect their energies along more thoughtful paths of action. In Chōshū it was the attacks in 1864 by the combined fleets of Great Britain, France, Holland, and the United States, precipitated by the domain's attempt to close the Shimonoseki Strait to foreign shipping, that convinced many samurai activists of the futility of opposing Western demands for commercial rights.

Word of such demonstrations of Western military strength traveled, and by 1865 it had combined with increased knowledge of the outside world in general to create a widespread acceptance among activists and officials alike that military reform was essential, and that in order to buy expensive ships and weapons foreign trade was imperative. What was more, to build such weapons a knowledge of science and technology was required. By this time, many military reformers were also ready to acknowledge the organizational needs of industry and finance, and some were beginning to speculate about the reorganization. It was the combined action of Chōshū and Satsuma that brought the latter phase to fruition.

Chōshū-Satsuma Alliance

As we have seen, these two outer domains, which had been vanquished in the battles that established the Tokugawa hegemony, emerged rapidly in the years after Perry's arrival to play the leading roles in the overthrow of the shogunate and the establishment of a new government. There were a number of reasons that impelled them to take the lead. As outer domains excluded from the central government and generally distrusted by the shogunate, they had a tradition of hostility toward the Tokugawa. Craig tells us of some of the ways this anti-Tokugawa bias was kept alive in Chōshū:

One ceremony embodying this animus was held annually on the first day of the new year. Early in the morning when the first cock crowed, the Elders and Direct Inspectors would go to the daimyo and ask, "Has the time come to begin the subjugation of the Bakufu?" The daimyo would then reply, "It is still too early; the time is not yet come." While obviously secret, this ceremony was considered one of the most important rituals of the han. Another comparable custom in a more domestic set-ting has also been recorded. Mothers in Chōshū would have their boys sleep with their feet to the east, a form of insult to the Bakufu, and tell them "never to forget the defeat at Sekiga-hara even in their dreams." In the case of Satsuma, every year on the fourteenth day of the ninth month the castle town samurai would don their armor and go to Myōenji, a temple near Kago-shima, to meditate on the battle of Sekigahara.[7]

Of more immediate importance than those formless thoughts of revenge was the fact that both domains were among the very largest in terms of productive capacity and both had an unusually large number of samurai. They were therefore ex-tremely strong domains, and their strength was enhanced by financial solvency. Chōshū for nearly a century had regularly saved a portion of its income and had invested it in profitable enterprises, thus accumulating capital that could be used in time of emergency. Satsuma owed its solvency to a highly profitable state-operated sugar monopoly. These resources contributed to high morale in the samurai class and enabled Chōshū and Satsuma during the 1860s to buy rifles, cannons, and ships. Without the 7,000 rifles that it purchased from the West, Chōshū probably would have been defeated in the second

[7] Craig, *Chōshū in the Meiji Restoration* (Cambridge, Mass., 1961), pp. 20–21.

bakufu punitive expedition. Still another advantage that favored the two outer domains was the fact that commercial development had not progressed so far there as in many areas more centrally located, and as a consequence class unrest had been less erosive of morale than in places close to the major urban centers.

For these reasons, as bakufu authority began to crumble, Chōshū and Satsuma emerged as the leading domains in the struggle to resolve the national crisis. At first they were rivals, each proposing its own solution to the crisis. Satsuma, as we have seen, became identified with the proposal of a "union of court and bakufu"; in 1862 it was able to win important concessions from the bakufu in the appointment of reformist officials, the moderation of the alternate attendance requirement, and the agreement for the shogun to travel to Kyoto to consult on national policy. Chōshū, on the other hand, put forth a rival and more extreme proposal for solution of the national crisis, favoring a more resolutely pro-imperial court stand and demanding the expulsion of the foreigners.

By the end of 1864 it became apparent to both domains that neither plan alone was satisfactory. After the shelling of its forts by the combined foreign fleet, Chōshū's leadership had to acknowledge the futility of expelling the barbarians. Satsuma, for its part, was dismayed by the bakufu attempts to assert its traditional supremacy in 1864–65 by reinstating the alternate attendance system, dispatching troops to Kyoto to establish control of the court, and gaining French technical assistance to build up its own power. In this situation, the antagonism between Chōshū and Satsuma was gradually overcome by their mutual interest in preventing a reassertion of Tokugawa supremacy.

In Chōshū, after the first bakufu punitive expedition, a civil war occurred that brought to power a new han government determined to press the struggle against the shogunate. The new government owed its triumph to mixed rifle units of samurai and commoners, some of which were commanded by former followers of Yoshida Shoin. When in August 1866 the bakufu sought to topple this new government and organized its second punitive expedition against Chōshū, it faced an army that was better disciplined and armed. Moreover, Satsuma this time refused to participate in the expedition, for the two domains had earlier that year concluded a secret alliance pledging mutual support. Chōshū's easy victory over bakufu forces obviated the need for overt aid from Satsuma. A year later, however, the two domains openly joined forces to administer the coup de grace to the demoralized shogunate. Acting in collusion with friendly elements in the imperial court, they seized the palace on January 3, 1868 and had the boy emperor, Mutsuhito (1852–1912; later known as the Meiji Emperor), proclaim the end of the Tokugawa regime and the restoration of imperial rule. In the ensuing weeks, Chōshū and Satsuma troops, now calling themselves imperial forces, engaged the bakufu army and, though outnumbered, quickly put it to flight. After two and a half centuries the Tokugawa Shogunate had come to an astonishingly sudden end.

The Significance of the Meiji Restoration

Much controversy has surrounded the Meiji Restoration, and the problems of interpreting its meaning have sharply divided historians. Should it be called a "revolution"? Was it motivated primarily by class interests or by ideology? What was the extent of Western influence? What was the relation between long-range socioeconomic change in the Tokugawa Period and the reforms that came after 1868?

If we were to look at the events up to 1868 and no farther, then it is possible to see only a coup d'etat—the displacement of one feudal group by another. Satsuma and Chōshū vanquished the Tokugawa, much as the reverse had occurred over two and a half centuries earlier. Thus Albert Craig concludes that "the Meiji Restoration was not a revolution, not a change in the name of new values—such as *liberté*, *égalité*, and *fraternité* in the French Revolution. Rather, it was what is far more common in history, a change carried out in the name of old values. It was a change brought about by men intent on fulfilling the goals of their inherited tradition. It was a change brought about unwittingly by men who before 1868 had no conception of its eventual social ramifications."[8] Studying the Tokugawa downfall from the perspective of Chōshū's motivation in joining Satsuma, Craig was impressed by the weakness of class consciousness, the strength of the vertical ties of samurai loyalty to the han, and the passive attachment of commoners to local political units. The morale of samurai in Chōshū was high. They were motivated to oppose the bakufu not by economic grievances but rather by their long-standing enmity toward the clan that had done in their ancestors centuries before. Craig concludes that "dissatisfactions . . . were not the sole or even the

---

[8] Craig, *Chōshū in the Meiji Restoration*, p. 360.

chief internal factor determining the course of the Restoration. On the contrary . . . the Restoration stemmed more from the strength of the values and institutions of the old society than from their weaknesses."[9]

If old values were strong in the outlying domains of Chōshū and Satsuma, as Craig contends, they were nonetheless weakened in many parts of the heartland, where the economic basis of the system had been transformed, where the problems of government were unsolved and morale was sorely tried. The fact that the bakufu structure fell as easily as it did and was not replaced by another feudal military government owed much to the debilitation and frustration that long-term social and economic change had wrought. The intense emotional reaction of the shishi to the bakufu's capitulation to foreign demands, and the dissatisfactions among peasants, inarticulate or backward-looking as they may have been, nonetheless were symptomatic of a disposition for radical change from the traditional social order. The restoration may have lacked, as W. G. Beasley says, "the avowed social purpose that gives the 'great' revolutions of history a certain common character,"[10] but the social consequences were nonetheless revolutionary, as we shall see. The samurai who seized power in 1868 rejected traditional proposals for overcoming the political turbulence that Perry had provoked, and embarked instead on a program that transformed the nation.

The strength of traditional institutions and values helps explain the restoration but not the revolution that ensued. Here most writers emphasize the nationalism of the new ruling elite, their determination to make whatever changes were required to restore national sovereignty. The motivations that initially inspired their campaign to destroy the Tokugawa gave way to recognition that traditional institutions were not equal to the tasks of national defense. It was as they acquired this recognition that the persuasiveness of the realist school of reformers began to influence their thinking. That pragmatic group, as we have seen, favored a positive government role in the production of capital wealth, the opening of the country to foreign trade, and the adoption of Western science. The young men who came to power in 1868 were mostly of lower samurai origins, who had risen in their han by dint of their high level of education and who were associated with many innovations, such as the employment of commoners in the militia and the establishment of

[9] Ibid., p. 353.
[10] Beasley, The Meiji Restoration, p. 423.

foundries, shipyards, and other strategic industrial projects. Although they lacked a clear blueprint for the future, the new Meiji leaders had many revolutionary attributes; experimental, open to the world, prepared to try new institutions and test new values, they were intent on reordering Japanese society and government.

The term "Meiji Restoration" is applied not only to the events leading up to the overthrow of the Tokugawa Shogunate, but also to the whole cluster of reforms that followed. For over two decades, from 1868 down to 1890, a series of reforms was promulgated that established constitutional government and put Japan on the road to industrialization. As they groped for alternatives to the old order, Japan's new leaders drew heavily for inspiration on the ideas and institutions of Western societies. Later we shall consider those institutional reforms and the beginning of Japanese industrialization, but we need first to discuss why Japan proved so open to new ideas and hence so responsive to the Western challenge.

One of the most extraordinary features of modern Japanese history is that sudden change in its view of the world. The Japanese as a people demonstrated extraordinary "intellectual mobility"—an unusual flexibility of thought, which allowed the predominant opinion of its leaders to shift very rapidly from xenophobia to xenophilia, from hatred of Western barbarians to adulation of Western culture. Some Japanese underwent a gradual metamorphosis in their world view; many others seemed to have undergone swift emotional conversions. It is often difficult to account for the rapidity with which attitudes were reversed. The new leaders of the government that came to power in 1868 had no clear idea of the extent of the reforms they wished to undertake, nor of the kinds of institutional changes they wished to make. But they did declare, in the Imperial Charter Oath, which they had the boy Emperor issue in 1868, that "knowledge shall be sought for all over the world, and thereby the foundations of imperial rule shall be strengthened" and that "all absurd customs of olden times shall be abandoned and all actions shall be based on international usage." These phrases signified a new openness to the outside world, and for the next two decades there

REVOLUTION IN JAPAN'S WORLD VIEW

followed a period of extraordinary borrowing, a period often described as one of intoxication with Western things and Western ideas. Where other Asian countries remained committed to their traditional knowledge and institutions, Japan undertook sweeping changes. A leading survey of modern world history concludes that this "Westernization of Japan" during the Meiji Period (1868–1912) "still stands as the most remarkable transformation ever undergone by any people in so short a time."[1]

In order to understand this sudden shift in attitude, it is well to remember that many Japanese "Westernizers" were in a manner anti-Western. For them, Westernization was a means to an anti-Western end: by adopting the techniques and institutions of Western society they hoped to eliminate all manifestations of Western power from their country. The jōi goal of expelling the foreigners, in other words, remained unchanged. (Although when we come to the 1880s and the craze for Western things reaches a peak—and we find Japanese leaders wearing top hats, studying ballroom dancing, going to masked balls with foreign ladies, and living in Western-style houses—we may begin to wonder just how anti-Western Westernization really was!) Essentially, the observation is valid that national security remained the object even during the 25 years after 1868, when Japanese leadership looked to Western countries for models of all kinds of institutional reforms.

Another frequent observation about the sudden reversal of attitudes is that Japan had a tradition of borrowing—of adopting and assimilating foreign culture to its own ends. In contrast to the ethnic self-sufficiency of the Chinese, Japan as an island country was keenly aware of the value of cultural assimilation in its history.

It is important to bear in mind as well the timing of the Western challenge. Momentum for change had been gathering for many decades. Had discontent not been so widespread, it stands to reason that the disposition to set aside many aspects of tradition would have been correspondingly less. But there was no great struggle to preserve the old order; it fell quite easily. The failure of the Tokugawa Shogunate to deal not only with its manifold domestic problems but with the foreign threat, which materialized in the first infringements of national sovereignty in Japan's history, prepared the way for change. The fact that the Western challenge coincided in Japan with domestic political revolution was exceedingly important: for those coming

---

[1] R. R. Palmer and Joel Colton, *A History of the Modern World* (New York, 1971), p. 600.

to power in such circumstances are free to make radical reforms in a way that people long entrenched are not.

Moreover, the nature of the new political leadership was of critical importance. The Meiji leaders were young: their average age in 1868 was slightly over thirty. They came out of the old samurai elite. As such they proved keenly perceptive of Western military strength and its basis in scientific and technological achievement. They were, therefore, more disposed to accept whatever changes seemed necessary to increase Japanese strength than was true, for example, of the scholar-gentry in China. The goal of national strength justified, in turn, a myriad of social and economic changes.

As a feudal elite they had not owed their position to the possession of a traditional body of knowledge, as did the Confucian literati in China. Hence, they felt much less threatened by Western learning. Nor were they bound to the past, in a social sense, so strongly as were many traditional elites. Their ties to the land had been broken in the seventeenth century when they had moved from the countryside to the new castle towns. Their power was rooted in bureaucratic positions rather than in landholding. J. W. Hall stresses that they "did not constitute an entrenched land-based gentry as in China, able to back up their interests in the face of modern change. Without an economic base, the resentment they felt toward the reforms which deprived them of their feudal privileges was soon dissipated. Instead, they were forced to ride with the times, to join the new government or to seek security in the new economic opportunities which were offered them. . . . In other words, they were a leaven for change rather than an obstacle."[2] Because they were free of the fear that most aristocracies have of losing land and property, the samurai proved remarkably receptive to new ideas and institutions. "Few ruling classes," writes Thomas C. Smith, "have been so free of economic bias against change."[3]

Fukuzawa and the New Westernism

No one wrote more persuasively or with greater influence on behalf of the new disposition toward wholesale borrowing from

---

[2] J. W. Hall and M. B. Jansen (eds.), *Studies in the Institutional History of Early Modern Japan* (Princeton, 1968), p. 187. Copyright © 1968 by Princeton University Press; Princeton Paperback, 1970. Reprinted by permission of Princeton University Press.

[3] Thomas C. Smith, "Japan's Aristocratic Revolution," *Yale Review*, L, 3 (1961), p. 379. Copyright © Yale University.

Western culture than Fukuzawa Yukichi (1835–1901). Japan's submission to the challenge of the Perry mission and to the subsequent demands for the forced opening of the ports was initially regarded as a political failure, for which the Tokugawa were blamed. As the magnitude of Western military superiority came to be understood, however, the failure was more often seen as a cultural one, requiring sweeping, fundamental reforms. Fukuzawa was the leading proponent of this line of thought.

Born into a family of lower samurai from the province of Buzen in northern Kyushu, Fukuzawa as a young man evidently chafed under the restrictions of the feudal hierarchy. In his autobiography he wrote, "the thing that made me most unhappy in Nakatsu [the town in which he grew up] was the restriction of rank and position. Not only on official occasions, but in private intercourse, and even among children, the distinctions between high and low were clearly defined. Children of lower samurai families like ours were obliged to use a respectful manner of address in speaking to the children of high samurai families, while these children invariably used an arrogant form of address to us." And Fukazawa went on, with typical modesty, "in school I was the best student and no children made light of me there. But once out of the school room, those children would give themselves airs as superiors to me; yet I was sure I was no inferior, not even in physical power. In all this, I could not free myself from discontent though I was still a child."[4]

His chance to leave Nakatsu came in 1854 when he was nineteen years old. It was the year after Perry's arrival, and Fukuzawa was sent to Nagasaki and then to Ogata's school in Osaka for the so-called "Dutch studies." Four years later he was sent to Edo by the han officials and ordered to establish a school for Dutch studies that other young samurai from his han could attend—the school that later grew into Keiō University. He soon learned English and in 1860 gained passage on a ship to San Francisco, which was part of the official mission going to America for ratification of the Harris Treaty.

While in San Francisco it was not so much the technological achievements that impressed Fukuzawa, for his years of Dutch study had acquainted him with the scientific principles involved:

Our hosts in San Francisco were very considerate in showing us examples of modern industry. There was as yet no railway laid to the city, nor was there any electric light in use. But the telegraph system and also Galvani's electroplating were already

---

[4] *The Autobiography of Yukichi Fukuzawa* (New York, 1972), p. 18.

The first Japanese embassy to the United States at the Navy Yard, Washington, D. C., 1860. *National Archives*

in use. Then we were taken to a sugar refinery and had the principle of the operation explained to us quite minutely. I am sure that our hosts thought they were showing us something entirely new, naturally looking for our surprise at each new device of modern engineering. But on the contrary, there was really nothing new, at least to me. . . . I had been studying nothing else but such scientific principles ever since I had entered Ogata's school.[5]

What fascinated him far more were social practices and institutions, such as relations between the sexes, family customs, life insurance, the postal and banking systems, hospitals, and lunatic asylums. On this and succeeding trips (to Europe in 1862 and to America again in 1867) he took copious notes on his observations. Fukuzawa first gained fame in 1866 with publication of his book *Seiyō jijō* (Conditions in the West), one of the most important books published in Japan in modern times. It was immensely popular because it described the kinds of everyday social institutions in Western countries that the Japanese were

[5] *Ibid.*, p. 115.

most curious about. In short order he published a number of sequels and became an established authority on the West.

Fukuzawa took no active part in the restoration. But when he realized that the new Meiji government was receptive to reform proposals, the whole tenor of his writings changed. Instead of merely recording information about Western society, he began vigorously urging the adoption of Western values and institutions and the fundamental transformation of Japanese culture. In his later books he went beyond the proposals of Sakuma Shōzan and others who had advocated adoption of Western science while preserving traditional values and social practices. Fukuzawa argued that one could not cling to Confucian ethics and acquire an understanding of Western science, because the former carried with it an attitude toward nature and society that was irreconcilable with scientific habits of thought. The essence of modern civilization, he contended, was found in the cultivation of individual qualities of independence, initiative, and self-reliance. Because he believed that the feudal system and Confucian values stunted those qualities, he made all-out attacks on traditional Japanese culture.

In one of his most important treatises, *Gakumon no susume* (An Encouragement of Learning), he began with words that became famous, "Heaven did not create men above men, nor set men below men," and thus succinctly summarized the revolt against inflexible hereditary status that had been brewing throughout the latter half of the Tokugawa Period. He went on to explain that a young man's position in society should be determined by his grasp of utilitarian knowledge. In *Bunmei-ron no gairyaku* (An Outline of Civilization), he located the fundamental flaw of Japanese culture in its basic institution—the family. By inculcating values of absolute power on the one hand and unquestioning deference on the other, the family had destroyed the spirit of independence that had formed Western civilization. He therefore, throughout his writings, attacked Confucianism, traditional education, and authoritarian government. As an educator, newspaper editor, and advisor to politicians, he exercised immense influence over the generation of Japanese that opened the country and rebuilt its institutions.

Agents of Cultural Revolution

To understand the responsiveness of Japanese society and the rapidity with which changes that led to industrialization and constitutional government were instituted, it is important to emphasize that the revolution was carried out from above, by a party from the traditional elite. As a result there was no great immediate social upheaval involved. There was no knockdown drag-out struggle between the old ruling class and a rising bourgeoisie, challenging samurai authority and demanding political rights. "There was no democratic revolution in Japan," Smith writes, "because none was necessary: the aristocracy itself was revolutionary."[6] The young samurai who came to power in 1868 carried out sweeping reforms that included doing away with the privileges of their own class.

The conversion of Ōkubo Toshimichi, one of the strongest men in the new government, illustrates the enthusiasm that many of the Meiji leaders acquired for full-scale reform. Ōkubo went abroad in 1871 with a government mission to make preliminary soundings of the possibility of revising the unequal treaties. What he saw in the West deeply influenced his thinking; England especially impressed him. He recorded his awe at "the excellence of the English transportation network with its railways and canals reaching into remote areas and with its well-kept carriage roads and bridges." Industrial enterprises in city after city affected him: the textile mills of Manchester, the shipbuilding yards of Liverpool, the Armstrong gun factory of Newcastle, and iron and steel works of Sheffield. Ōkubo confided to his traveling companions that before leaving Japan he had felt his ambitions were realized: centralizing power in the imperial government had been a great achievement. Now, however, he saw that many tasks remained, that Japan did not begin to compare with "the more progressive powers in the world."[7]

So he returned to Japan with new ambitions and threw himself into further reforms, inspired by the Western example, with a zeal that was especially apparent in his personal life. He began to adopt many of the trappings of Western civilization. With great fastidiousness, for example, he wore European dress, and was the first to appear at court with a Western-style haircut. He built a pretentious Western-style house, appointed with Western furniture, and boasted to his friends that "even foreigners to whom I have shown the house have praised it so I am quite pleased."[8] Daily he rode to the government offices in a fine two-horse English carriage. But more important, he began to

[6] T. C. Smith, "Japan's Aristocratic Revolution," p. 370. Copyright Yale University.
[7] See Sidney Devere Brown, "Ōkubo Toshimichi: His Political and Economic Policies in Early Meiji Japan," *Journal of Asian Studies* (February 1962), pp. 189–190.
[8] *Ibid.*, p. 191.

push national reforms beyond the limits of what he had earlier seen as his goals. Centralization of power in a new imperial government was not sufficient; Japan would have to carry out sweeping reforms of her whole society if she were to become the equal of the Western powers.

In addition to the industrial and military power that adoption of Western technology promised, another important motivation for Japanese cultural borrowing was the drive for national equality and respect. Ōkuma Shigenobu, one of the prominent Meiji leaders, later wrote that "to attain an equal footing with the other powers . . . has been the impulse underlying all the national changes that have taken place."[9] From 1868 to 1894 the prime goal of Japanese foreign policy was revision of the unequal treaties, so as to stand on equal footing with Western countries and escape the semicolonial status to which extraterritoriality and tariff control had relegated Japan. Leaders of the government concluded from discussions with Western diplomatic representatives that revision of the treaties depended not only on the development of national power but on legal and administrative reforms that would make Japan a "civilized" country capable of proper treatment of foreign nationals. The government moved quickly to plan such reforms. Committees appointed to compile penal and civil codes took French law as a model and engaged the French jurist Boissonade de Fontarbie to advise them in compiling laws. A German legal expert, Hermann Roesler, was entrusted with drafting a commercial code. As we shall see, the desire to impress Westerners with Japan's civilized progress was also a constant stimulus to the establishment of constitutional government.

The zeal for treaty revision elicited many bureaucratic efforts to reform Japanese customs. Government policy sought to modify traditional morality so as to avoid the criticism and disapproval of foreigners. Ordinances forbidding public nakedness and mixed bathing in public bathhouses explained that, although "this is the general custom and is not so despised among ourselves, in foreign countries this is looked on with great contempt. You should, therefore, consider it a great shame."[10]

Efforts to win foreigners' approval also included methods of artful persuasion. In 1883 the Rokumeikan, a gaudy Victorian hall, was opened in Tokyo so that government officials

---

[9] Quoted in Joseph Pittau, *Political Thought in Early Meiji Japan* (Cambridge, Mass., 1967), p. 39.
[10] Quoted in R. P. Dore, *City Life in Japan* (Berkeley and Los Angeles, 1958), pp. 159–160.

could entertain foreign residents with cards, billiards, Western music, dances, and lavish balls. Itō Hirobumi, the Prime Minister, gave a spectacular costume ball for foreign residents, in which he appeared as a Venetian nobleman and Inoue Kaoru, the foreign minister, as a strolling musician. It is clear from such episodes that the government leaders were pressing a Westernization policy not only as a means of strengthening the nation, but also as a part of the treaty revision effort.

A primary agent of the cultural revolution in the early Meiji Period was the new educational system. Education took on the burden of imparting a knowledge and understanding of Western culture and thereby preparing the young for occupations in an industrial society. The classical curriculum, which had already been modified in the late Tokugawa Period, was now almost wholly replaced by the study of Western languages, by scientific and technical training, and by a variety of disciplines whose content was adopted from Western education.

Japanese statesmen and intellectuals in the early Meiji period often looked back with contempt and distaste at the school system of the Tokugawa Period. Western-style education and Tokugawa-style appeared in sharp contrast in their minds. Fukuzawa was undoubtedly the most articulate advocate of the new learning, which he regarded as practical, scientific, and useful; and he was the most bitter critic of the traditional Confucian-oriented learning in Tokugawa Japan, which he regarded as stagnant, useless, and unprogressive. In a typical passage he wrote:

The only purpose of education is to show that Man was created by Heaven to gain the knowledge required for the satisfaction of his needs for food, shelter, and clothing, and for living harmoniously with his fellows. To be able to read difficult old books or to compose poetry is all very nice and pleasant but it is not really worth the praise given to great scholars of Chinese and Japanese in the past.

How many Chinese scholars have been good at managing their domestic affairs? How many clever men have been good at poetry? No wonder that a wise parent, a shopkeeper, or a farmer is alarmed when his son displays a taste for study! . . . What is really wanted is learning that is close to the needs of man's daily life.

A man who can recite the chronicles but does not know the price of food, a man who has penetrated deeply into the classics and history but cannot carry out a simple business transaction—such people as these are nothing but rice-consuming dictionaries, of no use to their country but only a hindrance to its economy. Managing your household is learning, under-standing the trend of the times is learning, but why should reading old books be called learning?[11]

This passage reflects the contempt that Fukuzawa and his contemporaries in the 1870s felt for traditional education, with its emphasis on single-minded study of the Confucian classics. Today, however, with the advantage of perspective, we can look back and see many valuable contributions that the Tokugawa educational system made to the efforts by Fukuzawa and others to strengthen their country and transform it into a great industrial power.

In the first place, the Japanese during the Tokugawa Period had experienced a vast educational network. In 1868 there were already about 17,000 schools of all kinds throughout Japan, ranging from the bakufu and domain schools for samurai to private academies and local schools (*terakoya*) for the commoners. Herbert Passin writes that at the end of the Tokugawa Period almost all the children of the samurai class attended some kind of school for some period of time, and that by the 1860s about 40 percent of male commoner children attended school. He estimates that attendance in the immediate pre-Meiji Period was about 1,300,000 children, and he points out that this figure corresponds almost exactly with school attendance in 1873, the first year of the modern school system. "Japanese were prepared for a modern school system because by the end of the Tokugawa Period millions of families had assimilated the routines it required into their mode of life. . . . In other words, the Japanese population was ready for the formal routines and disciplines of modern education because it had already had a long experience of learning in a setting of formal routines and disciplines."[12] The point is that the sheer presence of education as a widespread part of the environment, regardless of its content, is important.

In the second place, a much more apparent advantage that Tokugawa education bequeathed the Meiji Japanese was a high literacy rate. Passin estimates that by the end of the Tokugawa Period 40 to 50 percent of males were literate, a rate that compared very favorably with contemporary European countries. It made the Japanese a potentially highly skilled population, and as R. P. Dore stresses, it helped implant the idea of progress and the notion of self-improvement. Education was

---

[11] Quoted in G. B. Sansom, *The Western World and Japan* (New York, 1950), p. 454.
[12] Herbert Passin, *Society and Education in Japan* (New York, 1965), pp. 54–55.

sometimes a means of advancement in Tokugawa society, and it therefore created an emphasis on "achievement" and "ambition." By the end of the Tokugawa Period a desire to excel pervaded the schools. Dore provides an amusing example from a memoir describing how a boy and three of his dormitory friends in the 1850s engaged in a prolonged reading competition in a domain school: "We really went all out that month. If one of us got a page ahead the others would turn pale. We hardly took time to chew our food properly, and we drank as little water as possible in order that the others should not get ahead in the time wasted going to the lavatory—so keen were we to get a line or two ahead of the others."[13] The drive to excel, already far developed in late Tokugawa times, was surely in part responsible for the explosion of individual energies that characterized the Japanese of the Meiji Period and their desire to rise in the social hierarchy. A precept taught commoners in a local school makes clear how the ethic of achievement, reinforced by the threat of shame, was inculcated in children: "Illiteracy is a form of blindness. It brings shame on your teacher, shame on your parents, and shame on yourself. . . . Determine to succeed, study with all your might, never forgetting the shame of failure."[14] It is also worth mentioning, as Dore does, that the high literacy rate derived from Tokugawa education made the Japanese people more accessible to new ideas and new techniques, and it facilitated development of national consciousness. Both of these factors were important ingredients of the reforms Fukuzawa sought.

Finally, another aspect of the Tokugawa legacy that Fukuzawa and his contemporaries tended to forget was the fact that many of the things they advocated had already been developing in late Tokugawa times. Practical subjects, for example, had been given increasing attention despite a certain resistance by conservative Confucianists. Among the common people vocational education was widespread, and the shogunate and some of the important domains had already made major efforts in the development of technical training. The recognition of ability and special training, which was such an important underlying element of the ideology of early Meiji education, had already started in the 1840s. The heritage of Tokugawa education, therefore, was not so burdensome as Fukuzawa seemed to believe. In fact, an extensive modern educational system could not have been so readily established without it.

13 Dore, *Education in Tokugawa Japan* (Berkeley and Los Angeles, 1965), p. 211.
14 *Ibid.*, p. 323.

In 1871 the Ministry of Education was established, and the following year the Fundamental Code of Education was promulgated, emphasizing in its preamble that education should be universal and utilitarian. It set the ambitious goal that "there shall, in the future, be no community with an illiterate family, or a family with an illiterate person." It made four years of education compulsory for every child. Although that goal was not immediately realized, by the turn of the century over 90 percent of the children of statutory school age were in school.

The content of the new education was almost entirely drawn from the West. Dr. David Murray of Rutgers University was brought to Japan in 1873 as an advisor to the Ministry of Education. He and other American advisors were instrumental in the adoption of classroom readers that were almost direct translations of American textbooks, in the acceptance of coeducational common schools as the basic unit of the school system, and in the formation of teachers' colleges and vocational (particularly agricultural) schools. The number of foreign advisors and teachers hired during the 1870s is estimated at about 5,000. After the ban on Christianity was lifted in 1873, missionaries played a prominent role in the founding of new educational institutions, many of which later became colleges and universities. Principally by this vehicle, Christianity exercised a strong influence on the better-educated Japanese.

The new schools became agents of cultural and therefore social revolution. Success no longer depended on traditional skills acquired in the family; rather it depended on mastery of some aspect of the new learning, such as mechanical engineering, French law, double-entry bookkeeping, or English conversation. These were skills learned in the new schools—which were open to everyone. In this sense, "all Japanese," in Smith's valuable phrase, "were born cultural equals" in the Meiji Period.[15] The adoption of industrial technology created a great number of new educational groups, and professions opened up in industry, finance, journalism, education, and bureaucracy.

Education became the prime mechanism for social advancement. "Getting on" in the world, rising above one's father's station, became the consuming ambition of the "youth of Meiji." Japanese society thus became much more mobile. Young men longed to leave the countryside, go to the cities, and enter new occupations. Many youth from humble origins rose meteorlike to the heights of leadership in this freer society. That Samuel Smiles's *Self Help* was one of the most popular of the translated

---

[15] T. C. Smith, "Japan's Aristocratic Revolution," p. 383. Copyright © Yale University.

works in the Meiji Period was testimony to the emphasis upon getting ahead through hard work and ambition.

For a whole generation of youth in the 1870s and 1880s innovation and foreignness became vogue. As Dore writes: "Wearing a stovepipe hat, eating beef, forming a joint-stock company, using soap instead of friction, running committees by formal rules, planting new strains of wheat, consuming tobacco wrapped in paper rather than in a pipe, reading the Bible, adopting double-entry bookkeeping, sitting on chairs, were all parts of the new, Western, and, in the cant-phrase of the time, 'civilized and enlightened' way of life."[16] Many Japanese came to identify with patterns of Western civilization, believing them representative of universal patterns of development to which all progressive nations must conform. As Japan advanced she must inevitably become more like Western societies. Progress, in this view, required discarding traditional Asian institutions, customs, and patterns of social behavior. There was a general revulsion from an Asian identity. Fukuzawa wrote in 1885 that Japan should "escape from Asia":

Today China and Korea are no help at all to our country. On the contrary, because our three countries are adjacent we are sometimes regarded as the same in the eyes of civilized Western peoples. Appraisals of China and Korea are applied to our country . . . and indirectly this greatly impedes our foreign policy. It is really a great misfortune for our country. It follows that in making our present plans we have not time to await the development of neighboring countries and join them in reviving Asia. Rather, we should escape from them and join the company of Western civilized nations.[17]

This kind of alienation from Japan's own cultural heritage provided a powerful impetus to institutional reform in the generation after the restoration.

[16] R. P. Dore, "Latin America and Japan Compared," in John J. Johnson (ed.), *Continuity and Change in Latin America* (Stanford, 1964), p. 239.
[17] Quoted in Kenneth B. Pyle, *The New Generation in Meiji Japan* (Stanford, 1969), p. 149.

Much of the interest in Japan in the recent past has arisen from the fact that it has been the only non-Western society successfully to carry out an industrial revolution, that this was achieved with rapidity, and that the nation's economy in the postwar period recovered and advanced in an extraordinary fashion. The fact that Japan was able to achieve industrialization with a dearth of natural resources and with relatively little financial assistance from outside has further heightened the interest in its industrialization.

In this chapter we shall be concerned with the transition phase of the Japanese economy, the critical years from 1868 to 1885 when Japan mobilized its material and human resources and laid the foundations for modern economic growth. The great unsettled issue in the study of this period is that of determining the prime force behind the drive to industrialize. The part that government played in initiating the industrialization of Japanese society has been the subject of much discussion and controversy. There has been a tendency to credit the state with a larger role than it actually did play in the process. We shall see in the course of this chapter that private enterprise—the activities of individual Japanese—played no less critical a role than the state. What the government *did* do was to provide the setting for industrialization, to destroy old institutions that had proved obstacles to an industrial policy, and to create in their place new ones that would facilitate industrialization. It created the "infrastructure" of communication and financial institutions that was essential to the efforts of private entrepreneurs.

Initially, the most important contribution of the state was that the new Meiji leaders set economic growth and achievement of industrial strength as national goals. This decision was not something that emerged suddenly in 1868 but was, rather, the outcome of a long development that we have

BEGINNINGS OF INDUS-TRIALIZATION

briefly traced in the rise of the realist school of thought in the late Tokugawa Period. Adherents of the realist school, as we have seen, believed that government must itself adopt a policy of encouraging industry and commerce as a means of solving its own economic problems and of increasing its own strength. That policy gained support in many of the han toward the end of the Tokugawa Period, and the new leaders of the national government after 1868 effectively implemented it.

The State of the Economy in 1868

On the surface, Japan in 1868 appeared to have a relatively backward economy. It was still heavily agricultural, with approximately 80 percent of the gainfully occupied population engaged in farming. The American educator W. E. Griffis recorded in 1876 that he was amazed at "the utter poverty of the people, the contemptible houses, and the tumble-down look of the city as compared with the trim dwellings of an American town."[1] (He was speaking of the town of Fukui, where he spent much of his time.) This, however, was no ordinary backward economy. In Chapters 2 and 4 we discussed a great deal of evidence that pointed to economic change and development in the Tokugawa Period. As we saw, agriculture in many parts of the country was drawn into a well-developed system of national markets that encouraged specialization and stimulated productivity. Moreover, a goodly number of farm families were engaged in part-time nonagricultural occupations. A variety of cottage industries developed, such as brewing, ceramics, paper, food processing, mining, metals, and woodworking. As a consequence, many kinds of commercial and handicraft skills were widespread among Japanese farm families. The growth of the cottage industries reflected the rise and spread of attitudes conducive to economic change and development. In other words, probably the greatest resource that the Japanese economy had as it began its period of growth was a well-educated, economically motivated, and highly disciplined population. The growth of traditional manufactures during the late Tokugawa period had tutored this population in specific skills, attitudes, and commercial practices, which made it highly responsive to further economic development.

[1] Quoted in W. W. Lockwood (ed.), *The State and Economic Enterprise in Japan* (Princeton, 1965), p. 27.

While Griffis may have found the town of Fukui poor in comparison with the American towns with which he was familiar, other Westerners who had traveled more widely in Asia were impressed by the general well-being of the population, by the variety and abundance of goods sold in the towns and cities, and by the amount of traveling and shipping they saw. Townsend Harris, America's first diplomatic representative in Japan, wrote of the people of Kawasaki: "They are all fat, well-clad, and happy looking, but there is an equal absence of any appearance of wealth or of poverty." And of the population of Edo he observed, "The people all appeared clean, well-clad, and well-fed; indeed I have never seen a case of squalid misery since I have been in Japan."[2] The English diplomat Sir Rutherford Alcock wrote in 1859: "The evidence of plenty, or sufficiency at least, everywhere meets the eye; cottages and farm-houses are rarely seen out of repair—in pleasant contrast to China where everything is going to decay. . . . The men and women . . . are well and comfortably clad—even the children. . . . There is no sign of starvation or penury in the midst of the population—if little room for the indulgence of luxury or the display of wealth." In another location he recorded: "The impression is irresistibly borne in upon the mind, that Europe could not show a happier or better-fed peasantry."[3]

The economic historian Sydney Crawcour sums up his impressions of the economy in the 1860s as "reasonably, but not outstandingly productive for a traditional economy."[4] It was its potential and its responsiveness to economic stimuli that made the economy unusual. When exposed to the stimulus of foreign technology and foreign markets, the accelerated growth of the traditional economy made Japan's industrialization possible. During the Meiji Period the growth of agricultural output and of the production of traditional industries provided the capital accumulation that could be transferred to the modern sector of the economy by means of the land tax. This growth provided the exports which in turn gave the needed foreign exchange for buying raw materials abroad. Moreover, it satisfied the growing demands of the rising population. Therefore, traditional skills, resources, and their products provided the crucial building blocks for the foundation of a modern industrial society.

[2] *Ibid.*, pp. 26–27.
[3] *Ibid.*, p. 26.
[4] *Ibid.*, p. 44.

The Role of Government

Whether, in the absence of the stimuli of foreign markets and foreign technology, the commercial and agricultural development that was taking place in Tokugawa Japan would have led directly into modern industrial growth is a highly problematic and speculative question that need not concern us here. The steam engine did not have to be invented a second time. Industrial capitalism and modern techniques of production did not have to be invented in Japan. Instead, what was needed in the Japanese situation in the mid-nineteenth century was strong leadership, whether from the public or from the private sector, to mobilize Japan's domestic resources and to import the new technology.

In several important ways the government played a critical role in laying the foundations for industrialization. In the first place, it unified the administration of the country. This entailed a removal of restrictions that had impeded travel and commerce among different parts of the country during the Tokugawa Period. The old system of passports and barriers that had controlled traffic along the major highways was repealed, and citizens were now free to travel and choose their own place of residence. The new leaders strengthened the central government—for example, by abolishing the domains and creating a national army. In keeping with this unifying spirit, the government lifted existing feudal constraints on the internal market. The economic straightjacket into which the bakufu had put the economy was loosened, as a multitude of restrictions controlling commodity prices, the passage of commodities from one domain to another, and the operation of the market were removed. In addition, most barriers to foreign trade were withdrawn. The export of rice, wheat, copper, and raw silk, once prohibited, was now allowed.

Second, the new government also carried out a reform of the class structure. On the face of it, this was one of the most astonishing aspects of the Meiji Restoration. The party of samurai that came to power in 1868 proceeded to abolish the legal underpinnings that had made their class a privileged elite. The daimyo were handled without great difficulty. As we have seen, many of them had become merely titular leaders by the late Tokugawa Period, ineffective men whose actual power had long since declined. Moreover, many of the domains were in serious financial straits and the position of the daimyo was therefore one of considerable difficulty. Initially many of the daimyo were made governors of the newly established prefectures, and this helped ease any resistance. More important, they were given government bonds, and later titles, in the new nobility, which allowed them to continue to live with considerable means and prestige.

The new government likewise moved quickly to deal with the problem of samurai stipends and privileges. When the domains were abolished, it inherited the burden of paying samurai stipends, though it paid them at reduced rates. Nonetheless, between 1872 and 1876 stipends constituted anywhere from 25 to 100 percent of ordinary revenue, and it was clear that the new government, faced with competing demands for expensive western-style reforms, especially in military and educational matters, could not continue indefinitely to support a hereditary elite. Accordingly in 1876 the government commuted samurai stipends into interest-bearing bonds that would mature in 20 years, thus limiting and in the meantime substantially reducing the government's fiscal obligations. Meanwhile, the trappings of the old samurai elite were likewise cut off. Everyone was made equal before the law. Everyone was to have the right to a family name. Positions in the bureaucracy were thrown open to all classes. Former members of the samurai class were permitted to enter any trade they wished. The practice of sword bearing, the samurai's badge of social prestige, was ended.

Third, beyond administrative unification of the country and reform of the class structure, the most important institutional reform that the government carried out at this time to prepare the way for economic growth was the land tax reform. This was critical because agriculture continued for many decades to be the chief source of national revenue. To effect all of the reforms necessary for modern economic growth, government had to have substantial income and, for much of the Meiji Period, the land tax was the primary source. It was therefore vital that the determination and collection of this tax be modernized. During the Tokugawa Period the land tax had been collected nearly everywhere in *kind*, as a *fixed percentage of the annual harvest*. Not only was that method unwieldy, but also, because the tax was based on the amount of the annual harvest, it made it impossible to plan government expenditures in advance.

Between 1870 and 1873 a series of reforms was effected. First of all, land tax payments in kind were replaced by a uniform money payment, making this revenue independent of the price of rice. Second, the sale and disposal of land was made legal, thus giving formal recognition to a practice that had for a long time existed in one form or another. The landowners were made responsible for payment of the land tax and land titles

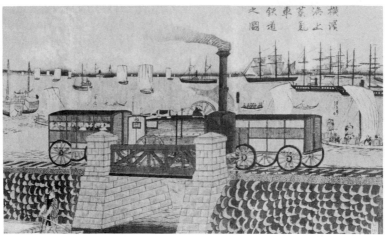

An early railroad scene near Yokohama harbor. The artist, Hiroshige (believed to be the third in his family), probably executed this print to commemorate the 1872 opening of Japan's first railway line, between Tokyo and Yokohama.
From the collection of Mr. and Mrs. Jack N. Greenman, Fort Worth, Texas

were issued to them. Third, to do away with the annual fluctuation in tax revenue geared to the state of harvest, the new tax was assessed according to the value of the land. The net effect of the reforms, therefore, was to establish a standard tax that would be paid on a regular basis in cash, thus providing the government with a known amount of revenue.

In addition to the administrative unification of the country, the reform of the class system, and the institution of the new land tax, government also played a critical role in providing prerequisites to economic growth by creating an infrastructure of communications, of public utilities, and of financial services. Moving very resolutely and effectively in these fields, the government by 1880 had succeeded in linking nearly all of the major cities by telegraph. Railway construction, which was, of course, more costly and technically difficult, proceeded less rapidly. A rail line was built from Tokyo to Yokohama in 1872; Kobe and Osaka were linked two years later; and in 1877 the latter line was extended to Kyoto. During those early years of railway construction the Japanese gained necessary technical know-how in construction, operation, and management of the railroads. As time went by, railway building began to pick up speed. By the turn of the century, nearly five thousand miles of railroad had been laid.

Also absolutely essential to future economic development were the reforms that the new government carried out in the field of currency and banking. The Tokugawa economy had been characterized by a chaotic variety of coin and paper money. One of the first achievements of the Meiji government was, therefore, the adoption of a new, standardized currency. In 1872 a modern banking system was begun with the issuance of the National Bank Act. It led ultimately to the establishment of over 150 banks, which depended heavily upon capital supplied by samurai commutation bonds. By the 1890s Japan had achieved a modern banking system with a nationally integrated structure of interest rates. Though the complexities and problems of establishing a modern banking system were by no means easily resolved, we may note here that, as with schooling, an accumulation of sophisticated techniques during the Tokugawa Period greatly facilitated the development of modern institutions. Even before 1868 many merchants were familiar with deposits, advances, bill discounting, and exchange transactions.

Of critical importance too, was the government's role in setting up an elastic and stable currency. In the late 1870s the economy was characterized by a galloping inflation that threatened to wreck the government's efforts to create conditions for modern economic growth. At this critical juncture the government was fortunate in having an extremely shrewd and astute finance minister. Matsukata Masayoshi was appointed to that office in 1881. For the next four years he pursued a financial policy of tight money and austerity, which produced "the most severe deflation of modern Japanese economic history." Matsukata, writes Henry Rosovsky,

combined firmness and wisdom with a strong belief in financial orthodoxy, and succeeded by 1885 in regaining control of the economic situation. He cleared the decks, and made it possible for modern economic growth to begin. . . . For five years he stayed on the same road, and by then the original government targets—adequate revenues, sound currency, modern banking —were safely and permanently achieved. The Matsukata deflation was strong medicine, but in our view it had life-saving qualities. . . . Thus, by about 1885–1886 the main targets of the government, first set in 1868, were in hand; a central bank was functioning, currency, purged of inconvertible paper, had become "respectable," and revenues were consistent with expenditures. It took government 19 years to accomplish this; from that time the economy was free to move progressively.[5]

[5] Henry Rosovsky, "Japan's Transition to Modern Economic Growth, 1868–1885," in Rosovsky (ed.), *Industrialization in Two Systems: Essays in Honor of Alexander Gerschenkron* (New York, 1966), p. 135.

The Role of Private Capital

We may discern two schools of thought regarding the prime force behind the drive to industrialize. Oversimplifying somewhat, we may term one the "growth-from-above" school and the other, which rose in reaction to the first, we may call the "growth-from-below" school.

The growth-from-above school holds that measures instituted by the government and by a closely associated small group of industrialists provided the major impetus. This point of view draws inspiration from comparative economic history, which tends to expect that in the early stages of economic growth strong government leadership is required. Alexander Gerschenkron argued from the examples of Germany and Russia that "the more backward the economy, the more the reliance on the state rather than on private enterprise." Adherents of the growth-from-above school stress the importance of the establishment of national banks, the government's role in importing technicians, sending students abroad, and investing in the industrial sector. In particular, they point to the role of official entrepreneurship in the establishment of model factories. Construction of modern cotton mills and the purchase of British spinning machinery by the government in the early Meiji Period set an example for private enterprise, by overcoming the initial ignorance of machine technology and factory organization. Then, once private inertia was overcome, these "model plants" were sold to private industry at low prices and on easy terms. Smith writes that without government help "Private capital would have been no more successful in developing machine cotton spinning in the decade after 1880 than it had been in the decade before; in short, in this field as in all others except silk reeling, the government was responsible for overcoming the initial difficulties of industrialization."[6]

To explain the motivation behind the drive to industrialize, many adherents of the growth-from-above school emphasize the patriotism and samurai spirit of the Meiji leaders and of the entrepreneurs who were closely associated with them. They argue that the traditional merchant class of the Tokugawa Period was largely lacking in the qualities of opportunism, inventiveness, and risk-taking that ordinarily characterize modern entrepreneurship. Instead, they find motivation arising out of the nationalistic or community-centered spirit of the old samurai

[6] Thomas C. Smith, *Political Change and Industrial Development in Japan: Government Enterprise, 1868–1880* (Stanford, 1955), p. 63.

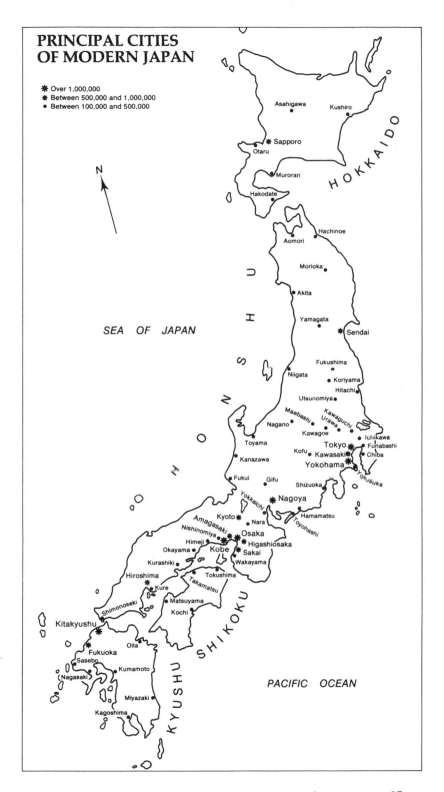

PRINCIPAL CITIES OF MODERN JAPAN

✳ Over 1,000,000
✱ Between 500,000 and 1,000,000
• Between 100,000 and 500,000

N

HOKKAIDO

Asahigawa
Kushiro
✱ Sapporo
Otaru
Muroran
Hakodate

Hachinoe
Aomori
Morioka
Akita
Yamagata
SEA OF JAPAN
✱ Sendai
Fukushima
Niigata
Koriyama
Hitachi
Utsunomiya
Kawaguchi
Maebashi
Urawa
Nagano
Kawagoe
Ichikawa
Toyama
Tokyo
Funabashi
Kanazawa
Kofu
Kawasaki
Chiba
Yokohama
Fukui
Gifu
Yokosuka
Shizuoka
Yokkaichi
Nagoya
Kyoto
Nara
Hamamatsu
Amagasaki
Toyohashi
Nishinomiya
Osaka
Himeji
Higashiosaka
Okayama
Kobe
Sakai
Kurashiki
Wakayama
Hiroshima
Tokushima
Kure
Takamatsu
Shimonoseki
Matsuyama
Kochi
Kitakyushu
Oita
Fukuoka
Sasebo
Kumamoto
Nagasaki
Miyazaki
Kagoshima

HONSHU

SHIKOKU

KYUSHU

PACIFIC OCEAN

85

class. As a result of their training, the samurai, in this view, possessed a selfless dedication to the nation that moved them to work for a wealthy, powerful country able to ward off Western imperialism. As one writer puts it, "in the case of Japan, the feudalistic samurai or their sons shouldered the leadership role of the Meiji entrepreneurs. Unlike any other nation, the development of capitalism was guided by bureaucrats who were samurai and by business leaders who were also of samurai origin. . . . Thus, the Meiji entrepreneurs were strongly motivated by the semi-feudal spirit of *shikon shōsai* (the soul of the samurai with business acumen)."[7] Why did Japan alone among non-Western countries make a rapid transition to industrial society? These scholars found the answer by pointing to the unique cultural tradition of its leadership. The spirit of bushidō —the warrior's code—inspired elements of the samurai class to selfless devotion to their nation, led others to invest their commutation bonds in the new national banks, and so fueled Japan's industrialization. In other words, the growth-from-above scholars stress a unique motivation behind Japanese industrialization—an "irrational, non-capitalist, dynamic and romantic approach of the pioneering entrepreneurs."[8]

On the other hand, the "growth-from-below" school argues that the traditional interpretation "overemphasizes the contribution of government and large-scale enterprise to increases in output, and that proper emphasis should also be placed on the contribution of the myriads of smaller rural and urban entrepreneurs who used more labor-intensive methods of production that embodied relatively simple improvements in technology, who acted in response to opportunities for profit, and who were relatively independent of the government."[9] These critics point out that the model factories were losing money when the government sold them off in the early 1880s and that afterwards, in the hands of private managers, they earned substantial profits. The conclusion drawn, therefore, is that private enterprise was not incapable of successfully developing modern industries.

Likewise these adherents downgrade the significance of the contribution of samurai to the beginning of banking. They point out that the commutation of samurai bonds was essentially

---

[7] Tsuchiya Takao, quoted in Kozo Yamamura, *A Study of Samurai Income and Entrepreneurship* (Cambridge, Mass., 1974), p. 214.
[8] Johannes Hirschmeier, *The Origins of Entrepreneurship in Meiji Japan* (Cambridge, Mass., 1964), p. 289.
[9] Hugh Patrick, "Japan: 1868–1914," in Rondo Cameron (ed.), *Banking in the Early Stages of Industrialization* (New York, 1967), p. 241.

passive participation—in other words, the samurai lacked alternatives for investment. Instead, these critics are impressed with the contributions of members of the old *heimin* (commoner) class. "While the participation of samurai in new banks was passive," writes Kozo Yamamura, "the heimin class participated actively in the majority of new banks by supplying the necessary cash (20 percent of the initial capital) and the entrepreneurial energy in the form of directors and initiators in obtaining charters."[10]

As a consequence of their emphasis upon the role of the commoner class, adherents of the growth-from-below school emphasize the profit motive rather than the peculiar patriotism of the samurai class. Studies of Meiji entrepreneurs par excellence like Iwasaki Yatarō or Yasuda Zenjirō, both founders of leading industrial combines, show them to be on many occasions cold, ruthless, competitive profit-maximizers—very much in the tradition of Carnegie, Vanderbilt, and Rockefeller.

Many of the Meiji entrepreneurs, it has been shown, emerged from the gōnō, the wealthy peasant class in the villages. The experience of their families had done much to prepare them for this new capitalistic undertaking. In the first place, they sprang from a tradition of leadership acquired in the villages, where many of their fathers had served as village headmen. Second, they had accumulated capital through investment in rural enterprises. Third, the experience in undertaking rural enterprises gave them qualities of initiative, self-reliance, and risktaking that the traditional city merchants in the Tokugawa Period had long since lost. Fourth, the gōnō were rendered both ambitious and frustrated by their position in the Tokugawa class structure. During the late Tokugawa Period, as we have seen, they had been able to share in the attributes of the samurai class—occasionally buying the right to wear swords, send their sons to fief schools, and take surnames. Yet they were not treated like bona fide samurai, and this experience was a frustration to them. They were therefore anxious to rise in the world, to be better than their fathers. Fifth, as a group the wealthy peasantry had always placed a high value on education and hard work. The interest in education, coupled with the wherewithal to acquire it, contributed powerfully to the emergence of young landlords' sons in the business elite.

An excellent example of this phenomenon is Shibusawa Eiichi, who rose from peasant origins to become the founder of

---

[10] Kozo Yamamura, "A Re-examination of Entrepreneurship in Meiji Japan (1868–1912)," *Economic History Review* (Spring 1968), p. 156.

several of Japan's impressive modern companies. His father was a village headman and rural entrepreneur who had invested widely in village industries such as indigo. Like many wealthy farmers' sons, Shibusawa received a samurai education. Through the good offices of a friend, he entered the services of the Tokugawa family and in this capacity accompanied a Tokugawa prince to France in 1867. When he returned a year later, having the extensive knowledge of the West that he did, he was able to enter the new Ministry of Finance in a prominent position. He resigned from the ministry in 1872 in order to enter banking and shortly became president of the First National Bank. His mastery of the field of banking led him ultimately into connections with over 500 diverse industrial enterprises in many different capacities, such as president, director, or major shareholder. One of Shibusawa's impressive early entrepreneurial achievements was in the field of cotton spinning. He imported the latest technology and in 1880 directed the construction of the Osaka spinning mill, which, owing to its up-to-date technology and efficient organization, proved extremely profitable. It became a model for the development of other successful textile ventures in Japan.

However the debate between these two schools is ultimately resolved, we may conclude that the government played an important role in creating the environment within which growth could take place. The establishment of a unified national administration, the mobilization of human resources, and the able use of fiscal policy were essential contributions of the state. Moreover, through what is now called "administrative guidance" (that is, through guarantees, subsidies, and preferential access to bank funds), the government used its influence to encourage economic growth. On the other hand, it is also clear that there was emerging a new breed of men in the private sector whose ambition, inventiveness, and opportunism contributed immensely to the expansion of commerce and industry in this period.

The task of building a modern nation-state engaged the Meiji leaders for the entire period of their hold on government, from 1868 through the turn of the century. The feudal organization of the country into over two hundred semiautonomous fiefs had to be replaced by a new political structure, which would centralize government and provide a unifying national spirit to galvanize the energies of the Japanese people for the tasks of building an industrial society.

Ordinarily, description of the process of nation building tends to concentrate on the formation of constitutional government, but in actuality the task was larger than simply establishing the Meiji Constitution. The fundamental task of the Meiji leaders was to mobilize the masses and integrate them into a new political system that would capture their loyalties and win their hearts. It involved a variety of techniques for mass mobilization and, above all, it required an effective ideology. Japanese scholars often refer to this process as the building of the emperor system.

Initial Problems

In contrast to the historical development of constitutional government in many Western nations, the Japanese experience was not one of a rising bourgeoisie bent upon achieving political rights. Rather, constitutional government was instituted "from above," the creation of a politically astute elite that had as its goal national power and equality with Western nations.

Within the loose alliance of oligarchs which controlled the regime in its early years, there was only limited consensus as to what kind of political structure should best be established in Japan. The oligarchy, which was composed chiefly of samurai from Satsuma and Chōshū (but included one or

BUILDING THE NATION-STATE

two from Tosa and Hizen, as well), had been united by their leadership of the anti-Tokugawa campaign but had achieved no more than broad agreement on the shape that political reforms should take. It took two decades of trial and error and struggle among them before the details of the new system of government were worked out. One step upon which all could agree was the need for administrative unification of the country. There was a notable consensus that until feudal divisions were done away with, essential reforms of the military, of education, and of the economy would be impossible. Accordingly the Meiji leaders, as we have seen, moved quickly to establish a highly centralized political structure. In 1869 the daimyo were induced to accept the title of imperial governor of the land they had held in fiefs. This was prelude to abolition of the domains and their reorganization as prefectures governed by appointees of the central government. The relative ease with which this centralization was achieved is comprehensible if we recall how weak most of the daimyo had become by late Tokugawa days, and how beset most domains were by fiscal troubles.

This unification, in turn, made possible the conscription law of 1873, which called for the replacement of the separate samurai armies of the many domains with a single national army based upon universal conscription. All able-bodied males, regardless of their social background, were liable for three years of active military service. The conscription law represented a decisive break with the past, which was required by the goal of building national strength.

Many of the oligarchs had come to the view that a hereditary elite was no longer consonant with national unity and efficiency of government. Itagaki Taisuke from Tosa, himself from a well-to-do middle samurai family, pointed out in 1871 how essential to national strength was the mobilization of the loyalties of all the people: "In order to make it possible for our country to confront the world and succeed in the task of achieving national prosperity, the whole of the people must be made to cherish sentiments of patriotism, and institutions must be established under which people are all treated as equals." To bring the ablest men into government, he said, it was necessary to do away with the old class divisions. "We should seek above all to spread widely among the people the responsibility for the civil and military functions hitherto performed by the samurai . . . so that each may develop his own knowledge and abilities . . . and have the chance to fulfill his natural aspirations."[1] Itagaki

[1] William G. Beasley, *The Meiji Restoration* (Stanford, 1972), pp. 384–385.

was not only summarizing the arguments developed during the Tokugawa Period for the promotion of talent, he was as well laying down one of the basic propositions of modern leadership.

After centuries of existence as a hereditary elite, the samurai had by 1876 lost all their exclusive privileges: superior education, possession of bureaucratic office, stipends, and sword bearing. The new government could not afford to continue supporting a hereditary elite, and it needed to cast a wider net for talent in administration. Inevitably, as the new government pressed ahead with its reforms, it engendered growing hostility among many groups of the dispossessed. The administrative unification of the country and the reforms that the government had carried out to put it on a solid basis were severely tested by several major samurai uprisings that occurred in the mid-1870s. Significantly, they all occurred in the southwest where the new Meiji leadership had emerged. The reason for this was that the uprisings were led by disaffected oligarchs—members of the original Meiji government who had withdrawn from it because of disagreements over policy, particularly disagreement over the extent of political reforms.

The government survived those challenges to its authority. But the final and by far the greatest of the samurai uprisings, the Satsuma Rebellion of 1877, required the full application of the new government's resources. The rebellion was led by Saigō Takamori, who had departed the government in 1873 over the Korean controversy. At issue in this controversy was whether or not to invade Korea, which had affronted Japanese sensibilities by rebuffing the overtures of the new Meiji government for diplomatic recognition. The controversy led to a fundamental division. A number of the oligarchs, including Saigō and Itagaki Taisuke, favored an invasion of Korea as a means of asserting Japan's national dignity and of giving vent to samurai frustration and energy. After protracted controversy their views were overridden by Ōkubo Toshimichi, Iwakura Tomomi, and others who had recently returned from Europe convinced of the primacy of domestic reforms. Ōkubo argued that war would divert resources badly needed to stimulate industry. He concluded that Japan must pursue a prudent foreign policy, seeking first to revise the unequal treaties, before undertaking bold overseas commitments. His arguments carried the day and set the basic course of government policy for the next two decades. Saigō therefore returned to Satsuma. He became the leader of a company of 40,000 disaffected samurai, who eventually rebelled in January 1877. By September the government's new national army had quelled the uprising, and Saigō took his own life on the battlefield.

The Movement for Constitutional Reform

Although such militant opposition was suppressed, the government still faced the challenge of other disaffected oligarchs, whose opposition took the form of the first political parties in Japan. Itagaki was the leader of the early party movement, known as the *Jiyū minken undō* (the People's Rights Movement), forming in 1874 the *Aikoku-kōtō* (the Public Party of Patriots). As we have seen, Itagaki had earlier argued that abolition of Tokugawa class restrictions was necessary in order to unify the people and to mobilize their energies for national goals. As a party leader, he now used very similar reasoning in arguing for creation of a national assembly, namely, that it would provide a means of marshaling the popular will in support of the policies of the state. He and his associates, initially from Tosa, resented the tight grip on power that the Satsuma-Chōshū group was acquiring. The constitutional order must be established, he asserted, to ensure that the will of the people was expressed through a representative form of government. For the next decade, Itagaki and his party, which was subsequently reorganized as the *Jiyūtō* (Liberal Party), invoked Western liberal ideas to attack the oligarchy and to demand the formation of an elective national assembly.

There has been considerable debate among scholars regarding the importance of the People's Rights Movement. Was it strong enough to compel the Meiji oligarchs to loosen their grip on power, to share control of the government with the people, to institute parliamentary institutions, and to begin the road to democratic government in modern Japan? There is no question that the Meiji government was compelled to take into account the demands of the opposition groups. Nonetheless, it would be wrong to think that the Meiji leaders were opposed to constitutional government or that they were forced to establish it contrary to their disposition. In fact, their interest in establishing a constitution and a national assembly antedated the People's Rights Movement. From the time of the restoration there had been among the leadership a keen interest in the idea of both a constitution and a national assembly. The Imperial Charter Oath, issued in April 1868, which set forth in broad strokes the outline that the Meiji leaders had for their future course, declared in its first article that "assemblies shall be widely convoked and all affairs of state shall be determined by public discussion." This article represented a general commitment to broaden the basis of government and to rectify the Tokugawa failure to consult widely about the formation of national policy. Precisely how this broader basis of government was to be achieved remained to be gradually hammered out through debate within the oligarchy.

Western political systems engaged the keen interest of the Mejii leaders and were carefully studied in the first years of the Meiji Period. Actually, the first students sent abroad by the bakufu in the 1860s, Nishi Amane and Tsuda Masamichi, had published their studies of the theories of parliamentary government, separation of powers, and the constitutionalism that prevailed in Western society. Likewise, Fukuzawa Yukichi's *Seiyō jijō* was influential in its explanation of the workings and theoretical basis of parliamentary politics in the West. Interest in Western constitutionalism was further heightened by the Iwakura mission, a group of oligarchs who went abroad from 1871 to 1873 to initiate negotiations with the Western powers and lay the groundwork for revision of the unequal treaties.

Constitutional government was regarded as an essential aspect of the treaty revision effort. Establishing a constitution would, it was thought, lend credence to the assertion that Japan was a civilized country with up-to-date political practices, perfectly capable of meeting the accepted standards of the nineteenth century. But more than that, a constitution and a national assembly were seen as a way of mobilizing Japanese loyalties and evoking popular identification with the new government. In other words, the institutions would in themselves be a source of national strength; they would interpret issues to the people, serving to transmit the wishes and goals of the central government. Furthermore, the assembly would serve as a safety valve for social discontent, allowing the ventilation of grievances through the participation of popular representatives in the central government.

Japan's new leaders, committed to the immense task of building an industrial society in the course of their generation, had to find ways of overcoming the disruption of vested interest, the social dislocation, and the psychological strain that this task entailed. They found in Western society no dearth of examples of popular discontent and even rebellion that had obstructed the goals of political leadership. They were therefore intent upon finding ways of spurring on the populace, of achieving national unity, and of preventing harsh antagonisms that would make impossible—or at least much more difficult—the task of building an industrial society.

The "Opinion on Constitutional Government," which Yamagata Aritomo, one of the leading oligarchs, wrote in 1879, illustrates the reasons why they favored constitutional government and a national assembly. While regarding political parties and other forms of opposition to the government as wrong and immoral, Yamagata believed that, in order to overcome divisions within society, popular estrangement from government, and economic discontent, it was necessary that the governed have the right to participate in national administration. "If we gradually establish a popular assembly and firmly establish a constitution, the things I have enumerated above—popular enmity towards the government, failure to follow government orders, and suspicion of the government, these three evils—will be cured in the future."[2] Yamagata, in other words, was setting forth what became the basic rationale among bureaucrats throughout the modern period for popular participation in government: the governed should be brought into the governing process not as a natural, innate right but rather as a means of achieving national unity.

Itō Hirobumi, who had emerged as one of the leading oligarchs by 1880, reflected a common view that ran through the thinking of most oligarchs about constitutional government when he wrote that "today conditions in Japan are closely related to the world situation. They are not merely the affairs of a nation or a province. The European concepts of revolution, which were carried out for the first time in France about 100 years ago, have gradually spread to the various nations. By combining and complementing each other, they have become a general trend. Sooner or later, every nation will undergo changes as a result."[3] There was a sense of inevitability about the establishment of Western forms of government. This feeling was a manifestation of the belief that Western civilization represented a universal path of progress. Just as those countries provided a pattern for economic and social development, so, it was thought, they provided a pattern for political development as well.

At issue among the oligarchs was the nature of the future constitutional setup and the speed with which it should be established. A critical turning point was reached in the so-called "Crisis of 1881." The issue was raised by Ōkuma Shigenobu, an oligarch from Hizen, who favored the immediate establishment of a British-style system with a cabinet responsible to an elected legislature. Ōkuma's proposal was rejected, and in a power struggle with the Satsuma-Chōshū group, he and his following in the Finance Ministry were forced from the government, but at the same time the remaining oligarchs came to a decision and

---

[2] Quoted in George M. Beckmann, *The Making of the Meiji Constitution* (Lawrence, Kansas, 1957), p. 130.
[3] *Ibid.*, p. 132.

Itō Hirobumi with his family. *Library of Congress*

publicly promised to promulgate a constitution and establish a national assembly by 1890.

Itō Hirobumi took charge of drafting the constitution. In 1882 he departed for Europe on an imperial mission to study the constitutional systems there and to collect material for the formulation of the Meiji Constitution. Although he observed practices in several countries, he was most impressed by the Prussian Constitution and its operation because of the evident similarities between the Prussian experience and Japan's own. In point of fact, it had already been decided prior to Itō's mission that Japan should adopt a Prussian-style constitution. So for that reason Itō, according to plan, spent the greater part of his journey in Berlin, where he heard lectures by the legal scholar Rudolph von Gneist over a period of many months. From there he moved on to Vienna, were he sought the advice of Lorenz von Stein, who reinforced the conservative views regarding parliamentary government that he had received in Berlin. "By studying under two famous German teachers, Gneist and Stein," he wrote to a fellow oligarch in Japan, "I have been able to get a general understanding of the structure of the state. Later I shall discuss with you how we can achieve the great objective of establishing Imperial authority. Indeed the tendency in our country today is to erroneously believe in the works of British, French, and American liberals and radicals as if they were Golden Rules, and thereby lead virtually to the overthrow of the state. In having found principles and means of combatting this trend, I believe I have rendered an important service to my country, and I feel inwardly that I can die a happy man."[4] The mission returned from Germany in late 1883, and thereafter Itō began work in earnest, drafting the constitution with the help of several advisors, including Hermann Roesler, a German legal consultant to the Japanese government.

The Meiji Constitution

The Meiji Constitution was promulgated on February 11, 1889. Although scholars since World War II have found fault with it and stressed its authoritarian aspects, the constitution nonetheless represented a great forward step for Japan in the establishment of representative institutions. It was greeted at the time with near unanimous acclaim.

The Emperor was the central symbol of the new political structure, and the constitution was presented to the nation as a "gift" from him to his people. The Emperor was to exercise all executive authority, the individual ministers being directly responsible to him, and he had supreme command of the army and navy. In addition, he had the right to suspend temporarily the Diet (the bicameral legislature), to dissolve its lower house, and to issue ordinances when the Diet was not in session. Only he could initiate amendments to the constitution. The Emperor was "sacred and inviolable" as the descendant of a dynasty "which has reigned in an unbroken line of descent for ages past." Sovereignty, in short, resided in him.

Separate legislation provided that the lower house of the legislature was to be elected by all males paying taxes of fifteen yen or more (approximately 5 percent of the total male population). The upper house, composed of members of the new peerage and imperial appointees, was to serve as a check on the lower house. The constitution gave the lower house the right to pass on all permanent laws and in addition the power of the purse strings; however, the government was given a loophole by which it could extricate itself from lower house control over the

---

[4] Quoted in Nobutake Ike, *The Beginnings of Political Democracy in Japan* (Baltimore, 1950), pp. 175–176.

budget. This loophole provided that were the budget for a particular year to go unapproved by the lower house, then the budget of the previous year would automatically go into force.

Basically, the constitution embodied the concept of popular political participation that had always been in the minds of the oligarchs: the national assembly as a means of achieving national unity. It was not a democratic concept, as was clearly indicated by the fact that the Emperor alone appointed ministers of the state, who were responsible to him and not to the legislature. The oligarchs spoke of the cabinet (which was not even mentioned in the constitution) as "transcendental," that is, as a body whose concerns and interests "transcended" the narrow, selfish political concerns of all groups in the state.

The New Nationalism

For the quarter of a century preceding 1890 Japan had passed through a time of unprecedented ferment, a time of experimentation and groping, as it sought to reorient its institutions to the realities of the international order into which it was so suddenly thrust. Building an industrial society had required supplanting much of the old order with techniques and institutions borrowed from the West. As the bureaucracy and the military, as commerce, industry, and education fell under the sway of Western example, there developed among the educated segment of society an intense ambivalence about traditional Japanese and the new Western cultures.

Such ambivalence, we have come to recognize, has been a characteristic problem of intellectuals in most late-developing societies, which must of necessity borrow new technologies and institutions from the advanced industrial countries. Under such circumstances, intellectuals are often strongly attracted to the progressive, scientific, and liberal aspects of Western civilization and simultaneously alienated from institutions and values of their own culture that suddenly appear outmoded. Yet, at the same time, building an industrial society is motivated by strong nationalist sentiments and therefore requires a strong urge for pride in one's own civilization. Nationalist sentiments and cultural pride were all the more intense in the heyday of imperialism, and admiration for Western culture the more perplexing because it was Western nations that offered the challenge to national sovereignty.

Many Japanese intellectuals argued that government policy in establishing Western institutions had gone too far, that it was demeaning to adopt the values and practices of Western civilization on a wholesale basis. As the articulate editor of a leading newspaper, *Nihon*, put it:

If a nation wishes to stand among the great powers and preserve its national independence, it must strive always to foster nationalism. . . . Consider for a moment: if we were to sweep away thoughts of one's own country, its rights, glory and welfare—which are the products of nationalism—what grounds would be left for love of country? If a nation lacks patriotism how can it hope to exist? Patriotism has its origin in the distinction between "we" and "they" which grows out of nationalism, and nationalism is the basic element in preserving and developing a unique culture. If the culture of one country is so influenced by another that it completely loses its own unique character, that country will surely lose its independent footing.[5]

On the other hand, there were many in the intellectual elite who saw the institutions of the West as representative of the road to national progress, who regarded Western values and institutions as of universal applicability. They tended to view cultural nationalism as reactionary. Wrote one editor, "We study physics, psychology, economics, and the other sciences not because the West discovered them, but because they are the universal truth. We seek to establish constitutional government in our country not because it is a Western form of government, but because it conforms with man's own nature. We pursue the use of railways, steamships, and all other conveniences not because they are used in the West, but because they are useful to all people."[6] The upshot of this "debate" in intellectual circles was a deep sense of uncertainty and restlessness. One young writer summed up the feeling when he said, "What *is* today's Japan? The old Japan has already collapsed, but the new Japan has not yet risen. What religion do we believe in? What moral and political principles do we favor? It is as if we were wandering in confusion through a deep fog, unable to find our way. Nothing is worse than doubt or blind acceptance."[7]

Government leaders recognized the problem, but they looked at it in a different way. They were concerned not so much about cultural pride per se, but rather about problems of maintaining order and re-establishing stability and unity in political life. They needed to mobilize mass support for the goals they

[5] Quoted in Kenneth B. Pyle, *The New Generation in Meiji Japan* (Stanford, 1969), p. 75.
[6] Quoted *ibid.*, p. 90.
[7] Quoted *ibid.*, p. 7.

had set for the nation. To provide the ideological glue that would hold the new political structure together, the Meiji leaders set about building an imperial ideology that would at once legitimize their rule and function as a binding and integrative force, enabling the Japanese people to act in concert and to deal effectively with their domestic and international problems. Itō put it this way:

What is the cornerstone of our country? This is the problem we have to solve. If there is no cornerstone, politics will fall into the hands of the uncontrollable masses; and then the government will become powerless. . . . In Japan [unlike Europe] religion does not play such an important role and cannot become the foundation of constitutional government. Though Buddhism once flourished and was the bond of union between all classes, high and low, today its influence has declined. Though Shintoism is based on the traditions of our ancestors, as a religion it is not powerful enough to become the center of the country. Thus in our country the one institution which can become the corner-stone of our constitution is the Imperial House. For this reason, the first principle of our constitution is the respect for the sov-ereign rights of the Emperor. . . . Because the Imperial sov-ereignty is the cornerstone of our constitution, our system is not based on the European ideas of separation of powers or on the principle enforced in some European countries of joint rule of the king and the people.[8]

To build support for the modern state they were creating, the Meiji leaders resorted to the traditional language of loyalty and obligation and drew on a mythical past to yield a distinctive national ideology. In 1890, just as the new legislature opened, the government issued a document of vital importance, the so-called Imperial Rescript on Education, which set forth the cardinal principles of this ideology. It exhorted the people to "be filial to your parents, affectionate to your brothers and sisters; as husbands and wives be harmonious; as friends, true; bear yourselves in modesty and moderation . . . always respect the constitution and observe the laws; should emergency arise, offer yourselves courageously to the State; and thus guard and maintain the prosperity of Our Imperial Throne coeval with heaven and earth."

In those Confucian terms the leaders set forth the concept of the family state, of the Emperor as the father of the nation and the subjects as his children. The rescript, which became a

---

[8] Quoted in Pittau, *Political Thought in Early Meiji Japan*, pp. 177–178.

part of daily school ceremonies, thereby equated political obligations with filial piety and sought to imbue the Emperor and his government with the sanctity and legitimacy that would suppress political opposition and dissent. As one scholar observes, "the Emperor became a substitute for the charismatic leader so prominent in the modernization of most nonwestern societies of a later period, a substitute that was more permanent, more deeply rooted in the culture, and more invulnerable to attack."[9]

At the same time as it issued the Imperial Rescript on Education, in 1890, the government began the conscious use of mass education to inculcate the new ideology. Textbooks, formerly only loosely controlled, became standardized and uniform —subject to the control of the increasingly powerful Ministry of Education. Schools, which in the early Meiji period had done so much to introduce Western concepts, now became a prime force in building nationalism, which was essential if the modern state was to evoke the self-sacrifice of millions of Japanese. Passages such as the following, in a school textbook of 1910, became common:

It is only natural for children to love and respect their parents, and the great loyalty–filial piety principle springs from this natural feeling. . . . Our country is based on the family system. The whole country is one great family, and the Imperial House is the Head Family. It is with the feeling of filial love and respect for parents that we Japanese people express our reverence toward the Throne of unbroken imperial line.[10]

In addition to the new national conscript army and the increasingly tight control of educational policy, another agency of centralization was the organization of local government, established largely as the handiwork of Yamagata. The purpose of the Town and Village Code of 1888 was to amalgamate over 76,000 Tokugawa hamlets into some 15,000 administrative towns and villages and so enable the central government to extend its influence into local communities, which had heretofore possessed a considerable degree of autonomy. By shifting loyalties from the hamlet, traditionally the object of identification for its inhabitants, to the new administrative towns and villages, Yamagata expected that material and spiritual resources might be efficiently mobilized for national purposes.

[9] Robert A. Scalapino, "Ideology and Modernization: The Japanese Case," in David E. Apter (ed.), *Ideology and Discontent* (New York, 1964), p. 103.
[10] Quoted in Wilbur M. Fridell, "Government Ethics Textbooks in Late Meiji Japan," *Journal of Asian Studies* (August 1970), p. 831.

To strengthen the new administrative towns and villages as an object of national loyalty, the government ordered in 1906 the merger of Shinto shrines and the establishment in their place of one central shrine in each administrative village. At the time of the merger order there were over 190,000 shrines in existence, the great mass of them small and devoted to the concerns of local inhabitants—healthy children, good crops, and prosperous communities. Communal spirits or deities (*kami*) were worshipped according to simple ritual that would elicit their protective powers. These local observances were the product of popular practices since prehistoric times. At the national level since earliest times the Japanese imperial line had based its claims to sovereignty on Shinto myths that proclaimed its descent from the sun goddess Amaterasu. The political authority of the imperial court was thereby sanctioned by the indigenous religion, and the Meiji government had at hand the deeply rooted traditions of the imperial cult, which could be elaborated and re-emphasized in the modern setting. The central bureaucracy sought to remold local folk religion into a powerful source of nationalism. Shrine liturgy was standardized to stress devotion to the Emperor rather than local concerns. Shinto priests were placed under the disciplinary rules of regular civil government officials. In the years immediately following the shrine merger order, a sharp reduction in the number of shrines throughout the nation was achieved. Important steps were taken in the creation of what we call in retrospect State Shinto.

By the early years of the twentieth century, the government was thereby succeeding in politically mobilizing the leaders of local society. Village headmen, elementary school principals, Shinto priests, prominent landlords, and other local activists were imbued with the national ideology and charged wth responsibility for achieving Japan's imperial destiny. They became interpreters of the national mission to the masses. As such, they played a key role in the national community that the Meiji leadership was disciplining for the forced march to industry and empire.

The 1890s marked a watershed for Japan. The mood and the concerns of the nation underwent dramatic change. During the generation after 1868, Japan had been preoccupied with domestic reforms, intent on reordering its society and government. By 1890, however, the new political order was established and a new sense of discipline and purpose was evident in the nation's life.

Most important in bringing about the transformation of mood and concerns was the Japanese entrance into international affairs in an unprecedented way. Since the restoration the prevailing policy had been to concentrate the energy and resources of the nation on domestic reforms and to avoid involvement in overseas entanglements. The primary goal of foreign policy had been to achieve a successful revision of the unequal treaties, so as to escape from semicolonial status, and that goal required concentration on domestic reforms. The policy bore fruit when, in mid-1894, the Western powers agreed to sign treaties providing for the end of extraterritoriality. Little more than two weeks after revision of the unequal treaties was achieved, Japan declared war on China and embarked upon its first great foreign adventure in three centuries.

The Sino-Japanese War of 1894–1895 was of immense importance in the history of international relations, for it revealed the full extent of China's weakness and set off an intense competition among the imperial powers for control of the resources and markets of East Asia. Japan was inevitably swept into this maelstrom and obliged to subordinate all its other concerns to the protection and extension of its interests. During the period from 1895–1915, which we shall concentrate on in this chapter, Japan emerged as one of the world's great powers, and the rise of its imperialism influenced nearly every aspect of the new industrial society that was taking shape in this period.

IMPERIALISM AND THE NEW INDUSTRIAL SOCIETY

9

Japanese Imperialism

Many factors were responsible for the strong imperialist drive that emerged in Japan at the turn of the century. The nationalist desire for equality with the Western powers was one important factor. Another was the economic motivation of maintaining access to the raw materials and markets of East Asia, which might be denied Japan if neighboring countries fell under the domination of one or another of the powers. Perhaps the most important underlying factor was the prevailing political instability of East Asia outside of Japan. In Korea and China, where Japan had the greatest economic advantage, old impotent governments were being undermined by revolutionary movements at the end of the nineteenth century. The impending collapse of these weak governments caused consternation in Japan because they might be replaced by Western control, with consequent jeopardy to Japan's security and economic interests.

By the end of the 1880s, as the Meiji political order was nearing completion, Japan's leaders were giving serious attention to the play of forces in the international environment. Yamagata and the heads of the military services had come to the conclusion that East Asia was likely to be the scene of fierce competition among the imperial nations. The vacuum of power on the continent invited it. Russia's decision to build the Trans-Siberian Railway confirmed their fears, for the new line would likely require a warm water terminus in Korea or South Manchuria. It became a cardinal principle of Japanese foreign policy that the security of the Japanese islands depended on preventing Korea from falling under the control of a third country. The General Staff, moreover, concluded that the "independence" of Korea could only be secured by control of neighboring Port Arthur and the Liaotung Peninsula. With those strategic objectives in mind, the government steadily built up the nation's military and naval power.

By 1894 intrigue and chaotic politics in Korea had created tense relations between China and Japan, each seeking to assert influence over the course of Korean politics. War broke out on August 1 and the superior planning and readiness of the Japanese military were quickly apparent. The war lasted only eight months. The uninterrupted successes of the Japanese army, the total destruction of the Chinese fleet, and the surrender of Weihaiwei persuaded China of the futility of further struggle. The Treaty of Shimonoseki, signed April 17, 1895, ceded the Pescadores, Formosa, and the Liaotung Peninsula to Japan, recognized Korean independence, and obliged China to pay a large indemnity, to open additional ports, and to negotiate a commercial treaty.

It was an immensely popular war, and greatly stimulated growth of the nationalist sentiment that the government had been seeking to promote through many of its new institutions. Victory brought the pride that had been wanting during the preceding decades of cultural borrowing from the West. As one young editor wrote in the midst of the war: "Now we are no longer ashamed to stand before the world as Japanese. . . . Before, we did not know ourselves, and the world did not yet know us. But now that we have tested our strength, we know ourselves and we are known by the world. Moreover, we *know* we are known by the world!"[1] Fukuzawa Yukichi expressed a common sentiment when he pointed out that triumph in the war had been a vindication of the Meiji reforms. "One can scarcely enumerate," he wrote in 1895, "all of our civilized undertakings since the Restoration—the abolition of feudalism, the lowering of class barriers, revision of our laws, reform of the military, promotion of education, railroads, electricity, postal service, printing, and on and on. Yet among all these enterprises, the one thing none of us western scholars ever expected thirty or forty years ago was the establishment of Japan's imperial prestige in a great war. . . . When I think of our marvelous fortune I feel as though in a dream and can only weep tears of joy."[2]

This new self-confidence, however, was almost at once deflated. On April 23, 1895 Germany, Russia, and France demanded that the Japanese government renounce possession of the Liaotung Peninsula "in the interests of the peace in the Far East." Too weak to oppose the three powers, Japan was compelled to retrocede the Peninsula. This event, known as "the Triple Intervention," made a profound impression upon the nation, underlining its diplomatic isolation and increasing its sense of insecurity. It became clear that Russian interests lay athwart Japanese ambitions in Korea.

The government set to work with a vengeance to expand military preparedness. Taxes were progressively raised as military expenditures more than tripled in the decade from 1893 to 1903. Yamagata wrote to a friend in 1895 that the situation in the Far East would grow worse and that Japan must be prepared for war in ten years with the Russians, who soon seized the southern part of the Liaotung Peninsula for themselves. Both

---

[1] Tokutomi Sohō, quoted in Pyle, *The New Generation in Meiji Japan* (Stanford, 1969), p. 175.
[2] Quoted in Kenneth B. Pyle, "Japan Faces Her Future," *Journal of Japanese Studies* (Spring 1975), p. 347.

Admiral Tōgō Heihachirō, naval hero of the Russo-Japanese War.
National Archives

the army and navy undertook long-term programs to build up their strength.

Meanwhile, to allow time for military preparation, Japanese diplomacy sought and achieved a modus vivendi with Russia. The agreement reached between the two countries in effect accepted a balance of their respective interests in Manchuria and Korea. Japan's economic interests on the Korean Peninsula were growing rapidly at the turn of the century. She was trading cotton products in return for foodstuffs and, above all, promoting an ambitious program of railway construction.

But the most impressive achievement of Japanese diplomacy was the signing on July 30, 1902 of the Anglo-Japanese

Alliance. For Japan the alliance not only overcame its previous diplomatic isolation, but also provided the first military pact on equal terms between a Western and a non-Western nation, thereby representing a great symbol of Japan's new-found respect among the imperial powers. The treaty, which promised British assistance if Japan became embroiled in conflict with more than one power, strengthened Japan's hand in its rivalry with Russia.

When renewed negotiations between the two countries over their interests in Korea and Manchuria broke down in February 1904, Japan went to war, beginning with a surprise attack on the Russian fleet at Port Arthur. The Japanese army, in a succession of battles in Manchuria, defeated but could not wholly dispatch the Russians. To finally crush the Russian armies would have required more resources than the Japanese possessed. Both the oligarchy and the army general staff were therefore prepared to negotiate an end to the war. The Tsar, however, hoped to turn the tide by sending the Baltic fleet around the world to overwhelm the Japanese navy. The Battle of the Japan Sea in May 1905, in which Admiral Tōgō Heihachirō's forces routed the Russian fleet, drew world attention. President Theodore Roosevelt wrote to a Japanese friend of Tōgō's triumph:

This is the greatest phenomenon the world has ever seen. Even the Battle of Trafalgar could not match this. I could not believe it myself, when the first report reached me. As the second and third reports came, however, I grew so excited that I myself became almost like a Japanese, and I could not attend to official duties. I spent the whole day talking with visitors about the Battle of the Japan Sea, for I believed that this naval battle decided the fate of the Japanese Empire.[3]

Roosevelt was subsequently persuaded by the Japanese to mediate between the two belligerents.

The war required an unprecedented mobilization of the nation's resources. The government mobilized a fifth of the male working population for some form of war service and sent a million men to the front. Casualties mounted to over 100,000 and the financial cost was immense. To sustain so heroic an effort, the war was justified as a great popular undertaking. Nothing in the nation's history had so heightened political awareness as this war. When the peace treaty was signed at

[3] Quoted in Shumpei Okamoto, *The Japanese Oligarchy and the Russo-Japanese War* (New York, 1970), p. 119.

Portsmouth, New Hampshire, in 1905, riots in many Japanese cities expressed the disappointment of the Japanese populace at the terms of the treaty and revealed their heightened political consciousness. Though the people had been led to expect much more from the treaty negotiations, Japan nonetheless emerged from the war with acquisition of the southern half of Sakhalin, the recognition of its paramount interests in Korea, the lease of the Liaotung Peninsula, and railway rights in southern Manchuria.

Historians usually describe the Russo-Japanese War as an event that brought Japan great power status and won her worldwide acclaim. It is true that the war does represent a landmark in modern world history: throughout Asia, leaders of subjected peoples drew inspiration from the Japanese example, believing that they too could import Western science and industry, rid themselves of white control, preserve their national character, and themselves oversee the process of industrialization. Jawaharlal Nehru, for example, recorded in his autobiography that the Japanese victory was a memorable event in his early life; he described it as "a great pick-me-up for Asia," which kindled his nationalism and his determination to "fight for India."

The attraction that many Asian leaders felt to Japan, however, did not survive the decade following the Russo-Japanese War. During this period Japan made very clear its expansionist intentions. Following the Portsmouth Treaty, Japan established a protectorate over Korea, and Itō Hirobumi was sent to Seoul to serve as resident-general. He hoped to carry out a benevolent modernization of Korea, which would gain the support of the Korean people as well as serve Japan's national purposes, but he underrated a nascent Korean nationalism. From the beginning of the protectorate, Korean resentment and resistance presented problems. Ultimately Itō himself paid with his life, assassinated by a Korean patriot in the railway station at Harbin in 1909, and the following year Tokyo annexed Korea into the Japanese Empire.

What is striking about this period is that, in spite of the fact that Japan seemed to have fulfilled the Meiji dream by revising the unequal treaties, joining the ranks of the great powers, and acquiring impressive overseas possessions, it was nonetheless beset by a keen sense of insecurity and vulnerability, a sense of the fragility of its position. The resources of the nation had been stretched taut during the war with Russia, and now there could be no relaxation even though hostilities had ended. The strategic requirements of Japan's empire were quite formidable. It included both insular possessions, which required a strengthened fleet, and continental territory, which required a strengthened army. From 1905 to 1914 soaring government expenditures for industrial capital formation and for military and colonial enterprises brought about extensive foreign borrowing, international payments problems, and a mounting tax burden on the citizenry. The political leadership faced an acute economic crisis.

The fearful demands that industrialization and imperialism were placing on Japanese society created a pervasive sense of uneasiness. The Meiji novelist Natsume Sōseki, despairing of the pace at which his country was driving itself, prophesied "nervous collapse" and admonished his countrymen not to be deluded into thinking of Japan as capable of competition on an equal footing with the great powers. The bureaucracy, however, was already hard at work organizing material and spiritual support for the mounting costs of government, trying to evoke the effort and self-sacrifice required for industry, empire, and status as a world leader. Bureaucrats in their public appearances explained that the burden the people must bear would not be lighter even though the war with Russia was over. A civil servant in Yamaguchi prefecture, for example, gave a speech several times in 1906 to local officials. Japan, he said, as a result of victory in the war, had joined the ranks of the world's first-class nations and had to expand its military and diplomatic establishments abroad as befitted its new status. It needed to invest great sums in industrial growth and education so that its people might develop the resources required to support the Japanese empire. The people had an obligation to contribute to the achievement of Japan's destiny by paying higher taxes. Although the shooting war was over, Japan was now engaged in economic warfare, which in some ways would be more trying than military combat. He spoke of the coming "peaceful war" in which every country would be Japan's enemy. If Japan's strength was to increase, the country must inevitably come into economic conflict with other countries. National unity would be imperative. Young men, old men, children, even women, he concluded, would be in the battles and must obey orders as in any war.

This pursuit of empire and of status as a great power colored all other aspects of Japan's national development. Most particularly, it affected the way in which the new industrial society took shape. A successful imperialist policy required a unified nation at home, with every part of society subordinated to the whole, with the state taking precedence over the individual citizen and over social groups. Leaders in business and government recognized that the new society as it came into being would disturb vested interests, create psychological strain, and cause social dislocation. If the drive for industry and empire was to be sustained, national loyalties would have to be continuously reinforced and every effort made to overcome the forces of disintegration.

The Problems of Industrial Society Come to Japan

Because of the timing of its industrialization, Japan experienced the social problems attendant upon that process in a much different context than did the "early developing" industrial nations of the West. As a "late developer," Japan had the opportunity to profit from observing the problems that the first industrializers had encountered and to try to avoid them. Marx wrote in the preface to *Das Kapital* that "the industrially more developed country presents to the less developed country a picture of the latter's future." What Marx, however, did not acknowledge was the possibility that the less developed country could, through the use of political initiatives, change the course of its industrialization and thereby avoid or mitigate the kinds of problems that the pioneers had experienced. Thorstein Veblen wrote in 1915 that Japan had a special "opportunity," by which he meant that by industrializing while feudal values were still strong Japan could avoid much of the social cost that had plagued other nations. Personal ties, vertical relations of loyalty and obedience, would permit a much smoother industrialization than if economic individualism took hold.

The Japanese leaders themselves, years before Veblen's essay, had shown that they were aware of the opportunity they had to benefit from the Western example, to try to plan a calmer and less searing transition.

We find, among Japanese bureaucrats and intellectuals a striking sensitivity to the lessons of Western history. We should learn, said one prominent official in 1896, from the "sad and pitiful" history of British industrialization. And, he added "it is the advantage of the backward country that it can reflect on the history of the advanced countries and avoid their mistakes."[4] The economist Kawakami Hajime urged in 1905 that Japan maintain a balance between its agrarian society and the new manufacturing sector, arguing that Japan could not survive the destruction of its agriculture:

[4] Quoted in R. P. Dore, "The Modernizer as a Special Case: Japanese Factory Legislation, 1882–1911," *Comparative Studies in Society and History*, XI (1969), p. 439.

Unfortunately, as the pioneer of the industrial revolution, England overlooked this great truth and that was probably inevitable in the trend of the time. But fortunately we have the history of England's failure and there is no need to repeat that history. Are there not opportunities for countries that lag behind in their culture? . . . The history of the failures of the advanced countries is the best textbook for the follower countries. I hope that our statesmen and intellectuals learn something from this textbook.[5]

For statesmen it was Japan's international position that gave urgency to averting the class antagonisms to which industrial civilization in the West had given rise. This was uppermost in the mind of one of the leading oligarchs, Ōkuma Shigenobu, when he wrote in 1910 that Japan was in an extremely advantageous position to secure the cooperation of capital and labor: "By studying the mistaken system that has brought Europe such bitter experience in the last several decades, businessmen, politicians, and officials in Japan can diminish these abuses." Relying on the force of laws and family customs, they would "prevent a fearful clash" and plan "the conciliation of capitalists and laborers."[6]

Thus, as Japan was making the transition to industrial society, her leaders were already thinking of the social problems likely to accompany the process. Their concern was made keener by the fact that European socialism was making its influence felt on radical intellectuals in Japan by the turn of the century. Following the Sino-Japanese War, a small but dedicated group of intellectuals and skilled workers tried to organize craft unions. The government, however, responded by passing the Peace Preservation Law of 1900, whose Article 17 outlawed strikes and other primary activities of labor unions.

As a result of the hostility of government, labor leaders after 1900 increasingly turned to politics. They became convinced that the regime would have to be changed, either peacefully or by force. In 1901 they organized the Social Democratic Party, which, although it did not have a long history—the Home Ministry closed it down hours after it was established—did attract attention to the new socialist movement and elicit the concern of government leaders. Denied the opportunity to organize effective trade unions or a political party, the young social-

---

[5] Quoted in Kenneth B. Pyle, "Advantages of Followership: German Economics and Japanese Bureaucrats, 1890–1925," *Journal of Japanese Studies* (Autumn 1974), pp. 129–130.

[6] Quoted *ibid.*, p. 130.

ists turned to methods of "education." In 1903 they established a newspaper, the *Heimin Shimbun*, which took strong and provocative positions against militarism, capitalism, and imperialism. In its pages was published the first complete translation of the *Communist Manifesto*. The newspaper opposed the war with Russia and for its pains was eventually forced out of business, while its editors were continually subject to police pressure. Frustrated in all their efforts, some of the socialists turned to anarchism and terror. Ultimately a number of them were implicated in a plot to assassinate the Meiji Emperor, and the government took the opportunity to move with severity to stamp out the anarchist movement. In the notorious "High Treason Case" of 1911, twelve radicals were hanged, three days after sentence had been passed.

As concern with social problems took root in Japanese intellectual and bureaucratic consciousness, the almost naive faith in the perfectibility of human society, which had characterized the early Meiji years, began to fade. Industrialization and imperialism put fearful demands upon society, and confidence in the future gave way to ambivalence. Every plus had its minus. The new technology was creative but also destructive; it offered new opportunities and prospects but at a high cost in human suffering and dislocation. As a result of the growing concern over the social problems that industrialization was likely to create, Japanese business and government leaders took the initiative in trying to prevent class hostilities, especially the alienation of the working class.

Origins of the Japanese Employment System

Recent studies of the Japanese factory system have called attention to several peculiar characteristics of industrial relations in present-day Japan, which have gained widespread attention owing to Japan's rapid economic growth. Many of these characteristics took shape during the period we are discussing, when the new industrial society was forming. It has been pointed out, first of all, that the large Japanese firm today has a low labor turnover—most employees enter a firm at the beginning of their working life and remain there until retirement. There is an understanding that the worker will not leave that company for industrial employment elsewhere, and, at the same time, the company will not discharge him or her, barring the most extreme circumstances. A second notable characteristic is the strong tendency of workers to identify with the fortunes of the company for which they work, to feel a deep sense of loyalty, and to organize unions according to their place of employment rather than by craft among many companies. Company unions, indeed, are quite common. Third, wages are determined more by seniority than by function or ability. In contrast to, say, an American firm—where wages are often related to the individual's contribution to efficient and maximal production—in the Japanese factory, economic rewards are most often determined by age and length of service. This characteristic naturally reinforces the low rate of labor turnover, since a worker is clearly penalized for changing jobs and conversely is strongly rewarded for stability. Fourth, Japanese firms provide notably high levels of welfare services for their employees. These include better sick pay provisions, retirement pensions, and a variety of other benefits, including housing, educational loans for workers' children, medical services, transport subsidies, and a variety of organized sports and social facilities.

Some of what we might call the paternalistic aspects of this employment system were, no doubt, natural outgrowths of Japan's cultural values, which stressed loyalty to the group and the extension of quasi-kinship relations to groups outside the family. While thus influenced in many ways by traditional values, the characteristics of the "Japanese employment system" crystallized in the early decades of the twentieth century because of several immediate factors. One was the continuing problem that employers had of preventing labor turnover—retaining skilled workers once they had been trained, at a time when the supply was limited. Because of the newness of the skills involved, the enterprises devoted great attention to the training of their workers. Once trained, such workers were at a premium, and great attention had to be given to preventing their leaving for other work. At the turn of the century, when the shortage of skilled labor was severe, the turnover rates ran between 50 percent and 100 percent per year. Workers would simply abandon one employer for another, seeking higher wages, better working conditions, and a different experience. As a result, to encourage long terms of service the new industrial employers began to extend to skilled workers a variety of incentives, such as retirement and sick leave benefits and regular salary increases heavily based on seniority.

Another factor encouraging development of the Japanese employment system was the growing awareness of the problems that industrialization had engendered in Western society. Labor strife, class divisions, worker alienation, social unrest, and the growth of radical ideologies were seen in Japan as inevitable products of industrialization unless leadership took steps to prevent them. The fact that labor organizations, strikes, and socialist groups were beginning to appear in Japan at the turn of the century reinforced this pattern of thought.

Because of the problem of labor turnover and because of the keen sensitivity to the Western experience with the social problems of industrialization, the larger firms, like Mitsubishi and Mitsui, took the lead in improving working conditions— such schemes as sick pay and retirement benefits, the establishment of the principle of "lifelong employment," salary increases according to seniority, and the development of profit-sharing bonus schemes—as a way to enhance the loyalty of employees. Large textile firms, with their reliance on the labor of young peasant girls, began to emphasize "familylike relationships" and the establishment of welfare programs. For example, Mutō Sanji, president of the Kanebo Cotton Textile Company in the early twentieth century, was a leader in developing a managerial ideology that emphasized paternal concern for employees and tried thereby to win their loyalty and affection. His welfare measures, Dore writes, included "a crèche [nursery] for working mothers, a workshop environment improvement fund with a claim to a percentage share of profits, much improved bathing and recreational facilities in the dormitories, an improved company housing scheme for married employees, subsidized consumer co-operatives for those living in company houses, a suggestions scheme, a complaint box grievance procedure . . . , a company news sheet . . . , a kindergarten to absorb the noisy children of night workers . . . and sick pay, pension and welfare fund . . . covering, for example, funeral expenses for members of the workers' family, paid by equal contributions from the worker and the firm."[7]

The government also became involved in measures that contributed to the development of the Japanese employment system. Leaders in the bureaucracy early in this century paid special attention to the practices instituted in Western countries to deal with the problems of industrial labor, and consequently they played an influential role in establishing welfare programs in Japan in hopes of forestalling labor unrest. As a result of government pressure, the first factory act was passed in 1911. It provided minimum standards for employment in manufacturing establishments with 15 or more workers. The impetus for this early legislation, it is important to note, came not from the laboring class or from pressure groups, but rather from bureau-

[7] R. P. Dore, *British Factory–Japanese Factory* (Berkeley and Los Angeles, 1973), p. 395.

crats in the Home Ministry, who had paid special attention to the development of factory legislation in Europe.

More important, the government also played an active role in trying to accommodate such differences as did arise between labor and management. In 1919, following an alarming number of strikes and much civil disorder, the government established the Conciliation Society, which promoted workers' councils and consultative committees as a means of co-opting the union movement and of channeling worker grievances. But perhaps the most important contribution of government was its propagation of the collectivist ethic throughout the nation. This ethic stressed vertical relations of loyalty and obedience, with a spirit of cooperation and self-sacrifice in all social groups. It generally set forth the concept of the "family nation," depicting Japan as distinct from the Western countries, where social unrest and class hostilities were described as endemic.

Agrarian Society

Agriculture played a critical part in making possible the emergence of an industrial society in Japan. By producing export products and substitutes for imports, it helped provide the foreign exchange that was necessary to buy machinery and raw materials from abroad. The growing productivity of agriculture in the Meiji Period likewise provided a needed supply of staples to feed, relatively inexpensively, the growing population in the cities. Moreover, agriculture contributed through the land tax a substantial part of the government income that built the infrastructure for industrialization and also a portion of the capital that developed industries. Because of the agricultural expansion, the transition to industrial society took place without a drastic lowering of the living standards in the countryside, which, had it occurred, would doubtless have been a threat to political stability.

Nonetheless, by the turn of the century the burden that agrarian society was bearing in the process of industrialization was becoming apparent and causing increasing concern in the Japanese bureaucracy. We discussed earlier in the book how the gōnō had acquired increasing amounts of land in the villages during the later years of the Tokugawa Period. The Meiji Restoration led to the confirmation of the landlords' position by giving to them title deeds to the property they had acquired. At the beginning of the Meiji Period approximately 30 percent of the cultivated land was tenanted. The increase in tenancy was aggravated by the land tax reforms of the 1870s, which, by requiring peasants to pay a fixed annual tax in money, worked hardship for the poor landowners, who frequently lost their lands by foreclosure. This was particularly true in the period of the Matsukata deflation (1881–1885). Therefore, the tenancy rate soared and by the turn of the century nearly 45 percent of cultivated land was tenanted.

Leaders of the bureaucracy sensed growing unrest in the villages as the gap between classes grew. Moreover, the increasing tax burden on the citizenry made the government particularly sensitive to the problem of villages. It must be remembered that at the turn of the century 80 percent of the population still lived in communities whose population was under 10,000. The government was, therefore, keenly concerned with preserving the cohesiveness of local society.

Indeed, without the material and spiritual support of towns and villages, the mounting cost of government could not have been borne. Requirements of armament, new colonial possessions, and industrial expansion caused central government expenditures to triple in the decade prior to the Russo-Japanese War, reaching 289,000,000 yen in 1903; they more than doubled in the course of the war, and then remained at just under 600 million yen down to 1913, by which time nearly half of the national budget was devoted to the army and navy, military pensions, and war debt service. Since the cost of the Russian war was over six times the ordinary revenues for 1903, extensive recourse was had to borrowing—particularly abroad. Taxes were raised, and lower- and middle-income classes bore an increasing share of the burden. There was some increase in the land tax, but the sharpest rise was in various excise taxes on such consumer commodities as textiles, kerosene, sugar, and salt. Indirect taxes rose from 96,000,000 yen in 1903 to 152,000,000 yen in 1905 and to 231,000,000 yen in 1908. Responsibility for public works and education was increasingly delegated to local government, causing local taxes to grow alarmingly and bringing their total to over 40 percent of national tax revenue after the turn of the century.

To strengthen the cohesiveness of local society and thereby provide a stronger basis for Japanese imperialism and industrialization, the central government in the decade following the Russo-Japanese War went to great lengths to shore up the administrative towns and villages that had been created through mergers ordered by the Town and Village Code of 1888. The government sought to strengthen them by encouraging the development of plans for improvement of landlord-tenant relations, by developing new crops and industries, and by reclaiming

Japanese schoolboys in 1905 study language textbooks. *Library of Congress*

land. In addition, the effort was being made to revitalize local
Shinto shrines and to focus their ceremonies on national loyalties revolving about the imperial throne. Campaigns to reward
"model villages" and "model headmen" were sponsored, and,
most important of all, the government sought to organize local
groups on a national basis. Youth groups, for example, which
had been organized within individual villages during the
Tokugawa Period, were now organized into a nationwide hierarchy (with a membership of three million by 1913), and great
emphasis was placed at all levels of the organization upon
national loyalties and devotion to the imperial cause. Local military associations were formed in nearly every village and again
were organized into a hierarchy under the supervision of the
army. They were instrumental in building respect for the army
and its values. These associations, established in virtually every
local community, numbered over 11,000 in 1910. Likewise of
great importance was a campaign by the central government to
encourage the formation of agricultural cooperatives. A law
regulating the conditions under which farmers could form credit,
consumer, marketing, and producers' cooperatives was enacted

in 1900. By 1913 the government reported the existence of over 10,000 cooperatives with a membership in excess of 1,160,000.

In this way, the central government reached down into local village society, to mobilize loyalties and to extend them to the national level. Of great importance, of course, in this effort was the rapid growth of school attendance. By 1900, 95 percent of the children of compulsory school age were attending primary schools. Here they were subject, as we have seen, to increasingly intense indoctrination in the new national ideology.

The emerging industrial society was thus shaped in nearly every way by political and military ambitions that Japan's leaders formulated for the nation. Landlord-tenant relations, moral instruction in the schools, allocation of economic resources, employer-employee relations—everything was to be subordinated to national greatness, to Japan's status as a first-rate power. The twentieth century, as the popular journalist Kayahara Kazan wrote during the Russo-Japanese War, "is not a time for individual heroes to vie with one another for fame. It is the time for national expansion and growth. This nationalism which has turned imperialism is now playing an unprecedented role in the drama of world history. Japan stands in the middle of this whirlwind, this ocean current of imperialism." Individual Japanese must devote themselves to the tasks of the nation, for Japan, he continued, "is destined to create an East Asian economic empire." This was "the ideal of a great people."[8]

---

[8] Quoted in Akira Iriye, *Pacific Estrangement: Japanese and American Expansion, 1897–1911*, p. 97.

The Meiji Period, one of the most remarkable epochs of modern world history, came to a close in 1912 with the death of the Emperor whose reign had witnessed Japan's emergence as the leading power in Asia. His passing was mourned by literati as well as by the masses, in a striking display of emotion that showed how deeply the new nationalism had touched the Japanese people. "A dense mass of humanity again thronged the great open spaces outside the Palace walls last night," wrote the correspondent for the London *Times*, "continually moving up to the Emperor's gate, there to kneel in prayer a few minutes and then pass on once more. The crowd was drawn from all classes, and all preserved the highest degree of orderliness and silence save for the crunching of the gravel under wooden sandals and the low continuous murmur of prayers. . . . One who looked over the sea of bowed heads outside the Palace wall could not desire better proof of the vitality of that worship of the Ruler. . . ."[1] Feelings were further heightened on the day of the funeral, September 13, when General Nogi, the military hero of the Russo-Japanese War, and his wife committed ritual suicide in the manner of the classic samurai who loyally followed his lord even in death. The most significant novelists of the time, Natsume Sōseki and Mori Ōgai, found that the emotional experience of these events changed the course of their writing. They were drawn away from preoccupation with the Western world back to their own cultural traditions for the thematic material in their subsequent novels.

The new Emperor Yoshihito, who gave the name Taishō to the years of his reign (1912–1926), was a weak and uncertain figure. It was a poorly kept secret that the

CRISIS OF POLITICAL COMMUNITY

[1] Quoted in Jun Eto, "Natsume Soseki: A Japanese Meiji Intellectual," *American Scholar* (Autumn 1965), p. 616.

Taishō Emperor's illnesses frequently involved mental aberrations. On one occasion while reading a ceremonial message to the Diet he rolled up the scroll and began peering, as through a telescope, at the startled legislators. Such behavior seems not to have diminished reverence for the imperial institution, yet it was perhaps symbolic of the nation's passage into a time of trouble.

This was not to say that the early years of the new Emperor's reign did not bring substantial new national achievements. The outbreak of war in Europe in the summer of 1914 provided extraordinary opportunities to advance the twin objectives of empire and industry, which the nation had pursued through the Meiji era. The preoccupation of the European powers allowed Japan to seize German holdings in Shantung and German islands in the South Pacific: the Carolines, Marianas, Marshalls, Palau, and Yap. More important, conflict among the great industrial nations meant that new markets and new demands for Japanese goods brought sudden economic expansion and prosperity. Exports nearly tripled during the war years, reflecting an unprecedented boom in industrial production.

But the period after World War One witnessed a succession of crises in Japanese society, and the problem of maintaining a stable political community sorely tried Japanese leadership. During the preceding fifty years the Japanese masses had slowly been awakened to political experience. By the first decades of the twentieth century it was becoming clear that they could no longer be kept out of political life. Industrialization and universal education contributed to this end; by the turn of the century there was a large number of newspapers and magazines designed for a mass audience. The increasing involvement of the populace in the issues of the day caused the leadership growing concern.

One result of this activation was that the political parties began to call for a broadened suffrage—ultimately, universal suffrage. Many of the Meiji leaders desperately feared this demand, believing that it would threaten the existing social order. Yamagata had warned his colleagues that universal suffrage would be tantamount to a socialist revolution. His fears were fed by evidence that industrialization was engendering new tensions and divisions in society: the labor movement grew more militant, landlord-tenant disputes multiplied, and radical groups proliferated. Those antagonisms were greatly intensified by the economic expansion during World War One and by the influence of socialist ideas from abroad. The basic question posed by events in the 1920s was whether the political system formed in the early Meiji Period had the resilience and the flexibility to absorb the newly awakening groups into its processes, and to accommodate satisfactorily the tensions and antagonisms of a burgeoning industrial society.

Evolution of the Political System

There is no question that the Meiji political institutions had the capacity to change, at least up to a point, for in the decades after the establishment of the new governmental structure in 1890 the system evolved in largely unexpected directions. The Meiji Constitution envisaged a political community directed by a small elite at the head of an extensive bureaucracy. In theory, this elite would consult public opinion as it was expressed in the Diet, but the elite would be fundamentally neutral, standing above the groups and factions represented in the legislature and acting in the interests of the whole nation. Although the Japanese state never lost its elitist character, the conditions of the several decades after 1890 created a much more complex and often unwieldy group that controlled the fortunes of the state.

The most noteworthy change in the political system was the growth in the power and influence of the parties. None of the oligarchs in 1890 accepted the idea of party cabinets. Instead they spoke of "transcendental cabinets"—made up of members of the oligarchy whose interest and loyalty supposedly transcended narrow party and factional interests and loyalties. Ito seems to have felt that party cabinets were possible some time in the distant future, when the parties had become truly national bodies; others, like Yamagata, saw nothing of the kind.

But all the oligarchs were wrong in their expectation that the parties could be circumscribed. There were several reasons why, almost from the beginning of the new Meiji constitutional order, the parties were able to develop new power. In the first place, while the elected House of Representatives lacked any legal control over the prime minister and his cabinet, it did have the negative power to withhold support from legislation proposed by the cabinet. More important was the veto power that the House exercised over the budget. Although the framers of the constitution had provided that, should the House prove recalcitrant, the previous year's budget would automatically come into force, in a time of rapidly mounting government expenditure, particularly at the turn of the century, this provision was little help. The Diet could greatly damage the plans of a cabinet by its refusal to sanction a proposed budget.

Although the cabinet had extensive powers to dissolve the Diet, it was forced to deal carefully with the parties and not to resort too often to arbitrary dissolution, else constitutional government would simply break down. The nation had invested its pride in making the new system work. Even after treaty revision had succeeded, the oligarchs were still anxious to demonstrate to the West—and to themselves as well—that they were equal to the challenge. As late as 1899, Itō remarked that "If there is one mistake in the progress and direction of constitutional government, there will be those who question the suitability of constitutional government for the Orient. This is what concerns me."[2] In short, it was a national goal that constitutional government should be made to work in Japan.

The lack of unity and the ambivalence among the oligarchs with regard to the workings of the new system provided opportunities for expansion of party power. Although Yamagata was in many respects dead set against concessions to the parties, Itō was willing to seek accommodation with them—particularly with the more moderate forces within the Diet. Moreover, the parties had already by the 1890s gained some measure of public support, which also provided stimulus for the oligarchy to meet some of their demands.

The parties went through a number of distinct phases in their gradual rise to a share in power. The first phase, from the opening of the Diet in 1890 to the beginning of the Sino-Japanese War in 1894, was characterized by implacable hostilities between the oligarchy and the parties. The latter posed repeated obstacles to the passage of government budgets, and the oligarchy responded by frequently dissolving the Diet. During the second phase, from 1895 to 1900, tentative short-lived alliances were struck between the cabinet and elements in the House. This was a time of rapid expansion of armaments, and the oligarchs were willing to make limited concessions to the parties in order to gain the passage of budgets. Those alliances, however, tended to break down once the oligarchs had won their way.

Nevertheless the realization was taking hold among the top members of the oligarchy that they had no recourse but to put such coalitions on a firm and stable basis. A third phase, therefore, of determined mutual accommodation between the two groups ensued from 1900 to 1918. This phase was inaugurated by Itō's decision to join a parliamentary party. In 1900 he accepted the presidency of the Seiyūkai (Friends of Constitutional Government) Party. In 1913, another oligarch and protégé of Yamagata, Katsura Tarō, followed suit by forming his own

---

[2] Quoted in George Akita, *Foundations of Constitutional Government in Modern Japan, 1868–1900* (Cambridge, Mass., 1967), p. 84.

party. It was during this phase that parties acquired the form and organization characteristic of Japanese conservative parties ever since. Having found party support indispensable to their power, the oligarchs now brought many of their followers in the bureaucracy into the parties they headed. Not only did the parties become "bureaucratized," but the reverse process was also taking place. Government agencies gradually came to be interpenetrated by party men.

In the working out of this process of accommodation between party and bureaucracy, no one was more important than Hara Kei (Takashi), perhaps the most astute politician in modern Japanese history. Hara, who had served in the bureaucracy but left it to pursue a distinguished career in journalism and business, helped Itō form the Seiyūkai and soon became the mastermind behind its emergent power. By making concessions to the Yamagata faction, which dominated the government in the early 1900s, Hara gained access to key appointments within the bureaucracy. The most important concession he could offer was Seiyūkai support for the budget of the government, which was particularly hard-pressed financially at the time of the Russo-Japanese War. In return, he had himself appointed to the office of home minister, a position that brought with it control of the entire network of local government, including power to appoint prefectural governors and to allocate government funds for public works. Hara used these powers to build Seiyūkai support at the local level. To potential followers he could offer local office and the pork barrel. He built up the strength of Seiyūkai supporters in the provinces by channeling resources to build dams, schools, and railroads in their areas. In the face of this growing power, other parties in the Diet were forced to coalesce out of self-defense, forming an anti-Seiyūkai coalition in 1913 called the *Dōshikai*, renamed the *Kenseikai* in 1916 and the *Minseitō* after 1925. In this development we may find the origins of two-party politics.

The stage was now set for a fourth phase in the development of the parties, which began in 1918 with the naming of Hara as prime minister. During this phase, which lasted until 1932, the parties attained a position of quasi-supremacy in the political system. That is to say, it became common during this period to give the prime ministership to the head of one of the parties. It was, of course, not constitutionally necessary (from 1922 to 1924 there were in fact three nonparty cabinets), but rather represented the acknowledgment by the elder statesmen (*genrō*), who advised the Emperor in the selection of the prime minister, that the balance of power in the political system had shifted in favor of the party elites. Their rise to power did not involve the parties' making a fundamental change in the political structure; instead, they succeeded in the shrewd infiltration and conciliation of the institutional forces established by the Meiji Constitution—the oligarchy, the bureaucracy, and the military. Since they were compelled by the constitutional order to turn inward for power, particularly to the bureaucracy, the parties did not become mass-based organizations. They built up their strength at the local level with men of influence who could be rewarded with office and with governmental benevolences. Nonetheless, this fourth phase seemed to optimistic observers to augur a trend toward the ascendancy of parliamentary politics and a growing influence of the common man over his government. Such observers therefore called this phase the era of "Taishō Democracy."

Turmoil in Society

The political parties gained their dominance at one of the most difficult periods in Japanese history. This was not auspicious. The parties, battling each other and seeking to maintain their position vis-à-vis the other elites, scarcely had the time or the objectivity required to resolve the multiple crises that wracked society in the post–World War One era.

The economic impact of the war had created a far more complex society than the one the oligarchs had sought to manage at the beginning of the twentieth century. Then, as we have seen, the bureaucracy had been hopeful that, by acting early before industrialism created the severe problems of Western societies, Japan could avoid similar unrest and conflict. Such sanguine views were quickly dashed in the postwar period. Social unrest, militant labor, and radical ideologies were all present for everyone to see. One could no longer speak of "prevention" and "acting early." The choice was now either to enact immediate social reforms to alleviate unrest, or else to resort to intensified national mobilization and suppression. The elites, gripped by a sense of crisis and fearful of social disintegration, usually chose the latter alternative.

The postwar period began with the Rice Riots in August 1918, when demonstrations swept the country in protest over a sharp increase in the price of rice. One source estimates that over 700,000 citizens participated in these riots, and in some of the cities troops were called out to quell the attacks on rice dealers and profiteers. Further evidence of the volatile nature of the people when aroused by social and economic issues came in the sudden rise in 1919 of labor disputes, numbering 497—ten times the number five years earlier. The number of labor unions mushroomed, and among the most important ones there was a trend toward radical thought and militant proposals. By 1920 the wartime boom was spent, a sharp recession had set in, and the nation began a decade of recurrent economic upheavals.

This unrest spread to the coutryside, ordinarily regarded as the foundation of a stable order. Yokoi Tokiyoshi, a leading spokesman for conservative rural values, had written in 1913 that in the face of rising radicalism in the city "we can only depend upon the peasants. The city will forever be a factory of revolution, while the country will always be the protector of the social order." Yet in the postwar period tenancy disputes became more numerous than industrial labor disputes, escalating from 256 in 1918 to over 2,700 by 1926. In some areas tenant unions were organized; by 1922 they claimed 132,000 members. Nearly half of the arable land was worked by tenants, and, particularly in areas where the number of absentee landlords was increasing most rapidly, the high rate of rents stirred resentment.

What in particular heightened the crisis atmosphere then was the extraordinary influx of radical thought. The Russian Revolution, the popularity of Wilsonian democracy, the growing alienation of intellectuals from the social order in Japan, and the unrest in society that we have just mentioned, all led to a striking diversity of ideologies that could not but be worrisome to government leaders. Their nervous concern was demonstrated, for example, by the hounding of a young Tokyo University professor, Morito Tatsuo, for publishing a rather innocuous article on the Russian anarchist Kropotkin's social views. In 1922 the Japanese Communist Party was established and became at once the subject of unremitting police repression. On the campuses liberal democracy and socialism were popular. The parties were not unaffected by those trends, and particularly among the opposition members, support for universal manhood suffrage grew. Hara Kei blocked such a proposal in 1920, confiding in his diary that enactment would have brought on revolution.

It is of course possible to exaggerate the extent of social unrest. For example, despite the signs of turmoil among industrial laborers, almost 60 percent of the industrial work force was composed of women, primarily young peasant girls who, prior to marriage, would work on short-term agreements in the textile industry. They were hardly the stuff of which radical labor movements are made. In fact, a sizable number of the male workers were fresh from the village and still imbued with traditional values of loyalty and obedience. In the countryside, despite the new unrest, it was still true that the great majority of tenants were not members of the tenant unions and were not involved in disputes. Even among the intellectual class, only a small minority favored radical change of the existing order.

Nonetheless, the ruling elites were fearful. Left-wing activities seemed incendiary, and there was no telling how high the flames of unrest might be fanned. Moreover, was not the revolution in Russia the product of only a small group of people? The situation was rendered even more critical by the great Kanto earthquake, which struck Tokyo, Yokohama, and the remainder of the Kanto Plain moments before noon on September 1, 1923. The intense shock brought the collapse of tens of thousands of buildings and the death of thousands, and far greater destruction was wrought by the fires that began everywhere in the aftermath of the quake. By the time the flames burned out, over 130,000 people were dead, billions of dollars of damage had been done, and more than half of Tokyo and most of Yokohama were laid waste. In the ensuing chaos and confusion, rumors spread that Koreans resident in Japan were committing acts of sabotage. Vigilante terrorism resulted in the slaying of thousands of Koreans. Matsuo Takayoshi, the most careful student of this pogrom, sets the figure at somewhere between 2,500 and 6,000 Koreans murdered. Police were involved in the slaughter, as they also rounded up scores of radicals. In one police station nine alleged Communists were shot to death; in another, Ōsugi Sakae, the leading anarchist, and his wife and nephew were strangled in their jail cell by a police captain. The paroxysm of violence left little room to doubt the volatility of the new mass society. As political leaders set about laying plans for reconstruction of the capital region, their apprehension over the social unrest was noticeably heightened. As a kind of aftershock from the earthquake, in December the Prince Regent Hirohito was shot at by a young radical angered by the anti-leftist violence after the earthquake. The cabinet that had taken office only the day after the quake immediately resigned.

Among the elite there was a division of opinion as to whether their proper, safest response to this unrest ought to be some kind of progressive adjustment of social and political institutions that would accommodate the new forces or whether, on the contrary, it was necessary to depend on a tightening authoritarianism that would control not only political behavior but also thought. The issue of universal male suffrage illustrated this division. When it surfaced in the first decade of the century, conservatives like Yamagata opposed it as destructive of the social order. Other leaders, however, saw it as a "safety valve" for unrest and believed that if the masses continued to be excluded from participation they would end up alienated and revolutionary. After the First World War the opposition Kenseikai Party took that position and used it against Hara, who opposed extending suffrage, fearing that it might weaken Seiyūkai power. Popular support for universal manhood suffrage continued to build, and many conservatives came to favor it, arguing that it would broaden political support for the state and contribute to national integration. In the days following the earthquake, the Seiyūkai decided to back universal male suffrage. It became law in 1925. At one stroke, the size of the electorate was made four times larger, numbering over twelve million.

In spite of their backing the suffrage bill, the conservative elites did not regard the prospects of a mass political community with equanimity. Rather they felt the need for further measures to limit the range of political debate and for intensified efforts to mobilize the populace to instill deeper commitment to national loyalties. Makino Nobuaki, an influential elder statesman, for example, said that universal suffrage would lead to social disintegration if it were interpreted as supporting egalitarian ideals. It was necessary, he concluded, to organize a league of all the semigovernmental organizations, such as the youth groups, military associations, and women's auxiliaries to cooperate with the shrines, temples, and schools in emphasizing national spirit and traditional values of respect for hierarchy and social harmony.

More important, the same session of the Diet that passed the new suffrage bill also approved by a vote of 246 to 18 the Peace Preservation Law of 1925, which greatly narrowed the range of permissible political debate by outlawing groups that sought to alter the form of government or to abolish the system of private ownership. In the ensuing years the police used this law to round up members of the Communist Party, their alleged sympathizers, and others of left-wing persuasion. Such pressure contributed to the weakness of the new leftist parties that were attempted after 1925, but those parties suffered as well from internal squabbling and from a certain intellectual orientation that divorced them from the mass support they sought.

The crisis atmosphere deepened in the latter half of the 1920s as the economy slid toward the depression. Government planners had been beset by recurrent economic crises, none of which were settled in a satisfactory long-term manner, with the result that chronic instability and a general malaise plagued the economy throughout the 1920s, exacerbating tensions and unrest in society. Policymakers had failed to restore equilibrium after the unprecedented surge of growth and inflation during the war. "The basic problem," writes Hugh Patrick, "was that prices in Japan had risen more than they had abroad; once the war ended, Japan was not able to compete sufficiently in international markets, despite the war-induced growth and diversification of her industry."[3] At the highest level there was a costly indecisiveness in dealing with this problem, with the result that growth lagged.

The small shopworker and farmer particularly encountered hard times. Agriculture stagnated and farm prices declined, because of both the import of cheap rice from Korea and Taiwan and the declining world market for Japanese agricultural goods, particularly silk. The recurring crises and government ineptness proved, however, but a prelude to the disaster that befell the industrialized world, including Japan, in 1929. The onset of the world depression brought collapse of the export market. Most damaging was the collapse of the international market for silk, Japan's principal export commodity and a product upon which most farm families depended for part of their income. By 1930 two-thirds of the net income produced in agriculture was spent on rents, taxes, and farm debt. Policymakers continued to flounder, compounding the effects of the depression by returning Japan to the gold standard at the end of 1929. Real farm income fell precipitously, with a calamitous effect on the standard of living in the villages. By the end of the 1920s social unrest in both cities and countryside had created a pervasive political malaise.

Weakness of the Political Parties

We have seen how the political parties steadily gained unexpected power within the Meiji constitutional system in the first decades of the century. They had achieved this position not by championing popular causes or by seeking reform of the political system, as some of the diehards in the parties would have liked, but instead by accommodating to the needs of the bureaucracy, by trading party support of government programs for positions in the bureaucracy, and by regional development projects that built up party support at the local level. This process of mutual accommodation opened the corridors to political power, and not a few writers in the 1920s saw Japan traversing the path toward political democracy that Western industrial

[3] Hugh T. Patrick, "The Economic Muddle of the 1920's," in James W. Morley (ed.), *Dilemmas of Growth in Prewar Japan* (Princeton, 1971), pp. 225–226.

nations had followed earlier. On closer look, this rise to power—that hardheaded realists like Hara had achieved—was bought at some considerable cost to the integrity and independence of the parties. Yet, to be fair, one may well conclude that, given the institutional structure within which the parties found themselves, there was no practical alternative to the course that they followed.

What characteristics had the established parties acquired by the 1920s? In the first place, they were not organizations with which the masses were affiliated or with which people could readily identify their interests and aspirations. Rather, the parties were highly elitist groups, membership in which required payment of dues, sponsorship, and the like. At the local level, therefore, their power was not in grass roots organization but rather in ties with district bosses, local officeholders, and families of influence whose loyalty and effectiveness in delivering the vote could be amply rewarded.

We should emphasize as well that the parties were not particularly ideologically oriented. The two major parties were broadly similar in their basic philosophy. While they might differ from time to time over practical issues they were fundamentally pragmatic and nonideological in character. By the 1920s the parties had lost the support of much of the intellectual community, which defected believing that the parties had grown so deeply enmeshed with the bureaucratic and business elites that they offered little hope of reforming the existing social order. It is true that the record of the parties' enactment of reform legislation, at a time which cried out for remedial measures, was unimpressive. There were, in fact, liberal elements in the bureaucracy that sought major reforms, but the Diet dragged its feet. In 1920 the Minister of Agriculture and Commerce established a research committee to deliberate ways of halting the growth of tenancy and thereby preventing the spread of "dangerous ideologies" and "class warfare." The committee drafted a liberal tenancy law, but it was scuttled by landlord interests in the Diet. Instead, a watered-down Tenancy Conciliation Law was passed in 1924 to help settle disputes.

The parties by their nature were heavily committed to satisfying the major interest groups—particularly the landlord and business classes. From the beginning, landlords had exercised great power in party headquarters, for they had the funds and local influence that party strength was built on in the provinces. The most notable phenomenon in the 1920s was the apparent degree of influence that the new business combines, the *zaibatsu*, acquired. Influence by industrialists within the government and the political parties was not new; it extended back to the early Meiji Period when, as we have seen, government played an important role in initiating industrialization and established close ties with the new captains of industry. What was new was the enormous concentration of capital that took place during and after the First World War. Nothing exemplified the dual structure of the economy better than these giant combines, highly modern and efficient, towering above the rest of economic society, which was still largely organized in small shops and farms. Zaibatsu like Mitsui and Mitsubishi encompassed a great variety of enterprises, including extractive industries, manufacturing companies, transportation networks, and banking and trading firms. The industrialists were a politically alert group, profoundly interested in many government issues, such as taxes and subsidies, patent and labor laws. They tried to control legislation by influence peddling—gift giving, entertainment, intermarriage with the other elites, and the like—and by financial support to the political parties. Bribery and other forms of corruption were widely charged against the parties in the 1920s. It is doubtful that Japanese political parties were any more corrupt than parties in the other industrial states, but the important point was their vulnerability at a time when quasi-Confucian suspicions of commerce were still alive and quasi-Confucian moral standards were still expected of the political community.

This brings us to a final and perhaps the most important characteristic of the parties, namely, their ultimate failure to justify or to legitimize themselves within the realm of Japanese values. The prevailing nationalist ideology stressed social harmony, selfless dedication to the state and society, loyalty and obedience to superiors. We have seen how government had taken that collectivist ethic, which had its roots deep in the cultural history of the Japanese people, and built it into an effective ideology to help overcome the strains of industrialism. It was inculcated in primary education textbooks and a variety of quasi-bureaucratic organizations—the youth groups, the military associations, and so on. But it was not something artificially bred and raised. In the village this ethic had never died out, but was still the way of life. Cooperation, deference to authority, conformity with the needs of the community, subordination of individual interests to the consensus, maintenance of harmonious relations with fellow villagers—these values remained of transcendant importance. As our discussion of the dual economy has shown, agrarian society had been *relatively* little changed by industrialization. In the 1930s over half the labor force was still employed in agriculture. Moreover, even in the cities the influence of the village could hardly be forgotten, for "three quarters

Coronation portrait of Hirohito, who succeeded to the throne in 1926.
National Archives

of the politically participant adults in 1930 were born in villages."[4] The government, therefore, had a broad base of collectivist values upon which to build an ideology that likened the state to a harmonious family with the emperor as the father figure.

In the face of such powerfully rooted ethical assumptions, parliamentary politics was always suspect. The hurly-burly in

[4] R. P. Dore and Tsutomu Ouchi, "Rural Origins of Japanese Fascism," in Morley (ed.), *Dilemmas of Growth*, p. 209.

the Diet of competing interests, majority rule, influence peddling, partisanship, and open conflict ran sharply against the grain of that collectivist ethic. It was one thing to accept the turmoil and tensions of party rule in "normal" times, but economic instability and social unrest mounted in the late twenties. Finally, there came as well a crisis in Japan's foreign relations. The result was a crisis in the political community that party supremacy could not survive.

The Meiji constitutional system had been predicated on organic unity and on the perseverance of shared values, i.e., the consensus among the bureaucrats, the military, and the Diet members. Prior to 1918 that system had worked tolerably well under the tutelage of the oligarchs, but by the mid-1920s they had disappeared from the political scene and centrifugal forces had weakened the pattern of leadership and decisionmaking that had guided the Meiji state. In the midst of severe social and economic problems, the political community was characterized by drift and a loss of mastery. What was more, the activation of the masses had added a disturbing new element to politics. Following the institution of universal manhood suffrage, the labor and socialist movements turned to the organization of proletarian parties, which, although they gained only 2 percent of the membership in the House in the 1928 elections, nonetheless were a source of concern in the midst of unrest and circulation of radical thought. This sense of drift and loss of mastery in the political community, in conjunction with a major crisis in foreign relations, set the stage for the demise of party supremacy and the rise of militarism.

Few countries in modern history have been as subject to forces of the international environment as Japan. The reasons might be endlessly debated. Some observers might attribute the fact to geography and to geopolitical factors that have made East Asia so tumultuous an area of the globe. Most would emphasize economic factors that have made the Japanese economy particularly vulnerable to changes in the international market. Others might point to cultural factors that have rendered the Japanese peculiarly receptive to foreign influences and trends. Still others would emphasize historical contingencies and the particular timing of Japan's emergence from isolation, which came with the arrival of Western power and imperialism in the Pacific.

Whatever the causes, Japan has been ceaselessly buffeted by outside forces and its modern history uniquely shaped by them. During most of this time the nation moved cautiously, ever sensitive to such currents of power politics and cultural development. The leaders of Japan sought to use those currents, to capitalize on those trends by moving with them, with circumspection seeking to turn them to its advantage, and in this prudent fashion to achieve its national ambitions.

From the time of the restoration down to the 1930s, Japan was motivated by a sense of insecurity, both physical and cultural, and by ambition for national power, respect, and equality. Those motives, intertwined and often inseparable, made up the peculiar nationalism that impelled its historical advance. Japanese diplomacy was remarkable for the way in which it sought to pursue those national ambitions by accommodating to the international system, as the leaders understood it. Thus, for example, during the first twenty-five years of the Meiji Period, revision of the unequal treaties was pursued by determinedly adopting European legal institutions and usages. With rare, isolated

THE MILITARIST ERA

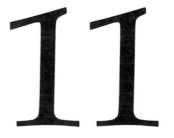

exceptions, that pattern of approach continued to guide Japanese diplomats. Only in the militarist era of the 1930s, to which we now turn, did Japan appear to abandon that circumspection, to assert willfully its own way in international affairs and attempt to establish its own destiny in defiance of the forces rising up against it.

Ending of the Imperialist System

World War One was to transform the international system in East Asia, much as it would transform the context of Japanese domestic politics. On the eve of the war, a stable order apparently prevailed among the imperial powers, after two decades of struggle. Finding itself isolated and outmaneuvered in the Triple Intervention of 1895, Japan had worked its way into the power structure by using skillful diplomacy, backed on occasion by military force. The Anglo-Japanese Alliance of 1902 established a pattern of cooperation with Britain and contributed to the development of an understanding with the United States. In a series of agreements, the latter acknowledged Japan's position in Northeast Asia, in 1905 acquiescing to the Japanese protectorate of Korea. At the same time, Russia and Japan had by war delimited their spheres of interest, with the former now relegated to protecting its remaining hold on northern Manchuria. The "system" was in rough equilibrium by this time, with the interests of each power more or less acknowledged: the United States in the Philippines, France in Indochina, Britain in the Yangtze Valley and in South China, Germany in the Shantung Peninsula, and Russia and Japan in Northeast Asia.

World War One upset this balance, and eventually the East Asian power structure collapsed. The outbreak of war in Europe in the summer of 1914 and the preoccupation of the European powers allowed Japan, under the guise of the Anglo-Japanese Alliance, to seize German holdings in Shantung and German-held islands in the South Pacific: the Carolines, Marianas, Marshalls, Palau, and Yap. Hard on the heels of those swift maneuvers came the delivery in January 1915 of Japan's Twenty-One Demands on China. This was an incident fraught with importance for the future of international relations in East Asia: first, because it was interpreted as a unilateral departure from the system of understanding developed among the powers in the preceding two decades; and second, because it marked a growing Japanese-American estrangement and the emergence of the United States' role as protector of the new Chinese Republic.

The Twenty-One Demands sought Chinese recognition of the transference of German rights in Shantung to Japan; the employment of Japanese nationals as political, financial, and military advisors in China; Chinese purchase of arms from Japan; and permission for Japan to construct railways connecting the Yangtze Valley with the South China coast. The demands elicited a sharp reaction in England and even more so in the United States, where President Woodrow Wilson reached the conclusion that the American people must be "champions of the sovereign rights of China." What was more, there was dissension within the Japanese government, particularly among the elder statesmen or genrō, who had not been included in the planning of the demands and who opposed the kind of diplomacy that needlessly riled the powers and damaged the Japanese image in China. Yamagata was especially disturbed, having warned a year earlier that "if we fail to dissipate China's suspicion of us, [it] will rapidly turn against us and turn more and more to America."[1] The Japanese government subsequently modified the demands, but the episode augured ill for Sino-Japanese relations and prefigured the problems that beset Japanese-American relations in the 1930s. For the nascent Chinese nationalist movement, the Twenty-One Demands stood as a symbol of Japan's predatory designs and, as Yamagata had feared, nationalism took on an increasing anti-Japanese tone in the aftermath.

It is of course possible to date the origins of the Japanese-American estrangement a decade earlier, in the tensions that developed after the Russo-Japanese War. In part the estrangement grew from racial friction raised by immigration to the West Coast. In 1905 the California legislature had unanimously passed a resolution calling on the government to limit immigration, and characterizing Japanese immigrants as "immoral, intemperate, quarrelsome men bound to labor for a pittance." The following year the San Francisco School Board set up an Oriental Public School for Japanese, Korean, and Chinese children. A "gentlemen's agreement" was worked out to resolve the crisis, whereby the school board rescinded its order and the Japanese government took it upon itself to prevent the issuance of visas to laborers bound for the mainland United States. But the inci-

---

[1] Quoted in Marius B. Jansen, *Japan and China: From War to Peace, 1894–1972* (Chicago, 1975), p. 202.

dents were frequently interpreted in the Japanese press as fresh evidence that Japan was still not accepted on an equal footing with the Western powers. The animosities aroused by those events also called attention to the potential conflict of interests of the two countries in the Pacific. The military in both countries, as a consequence, began to pay more attention to the relative strength of each other's armaments and to the possibility of a military encounter.

The clash of interests was, however, more sharply drawn by the Twenty-One Demands, for subsequent to their presentation the United States made clear its intention of maintaining an Open Door for American trade and investment in China and its growing opposition to Japan's continental aspirations. Wilson's "new diplomacy" proclaimed self-determination and the sovereign rights of every people, and from the time of the demands he made increasingly plain his opposition to international power rivalries at China's expense.

The issues raised by the immigration problem and by the Twenty-One Demands reappeared at the Paris Peace Conference in 1919. Wilson was deeply embarrassed over his failure to support the Japanese request that a racial equality clause be inserted in the League of Nations Covenant, which would state "that the principle of equality of nations and the just treatment of their nationals . . . [shall be] a fundamental basis of future international relations in the new world organization." The Anglo-American powers, fearful of its implications as to immigration, abstained from voting on the proposal, which was equivalent to voting against it. For the Japanese delegation, which included a number of future prime ministers and foreign ministers (Konoe Fumimaro, Matsuoka Yōsuke, Shigemitsu Mamoru, and Yoshida Shigeru), it was interpreted as another painful reminder that they were still not accepted by the Western world.

Though the principles of the "new diplomacy" were primarily intended for Europe, Wilson wanted to apply them to Asia as well and spare China further buffeting. He told his European counterparts at the Paris conference that "there was nothing on which the public opinion of the United States of America was firmer than on this question that China should not be oppressed by Japan."[2] The balance of power among the imperialists in East Asia would have to be replaced by a new order, in which all would refrain from military and political expansion. The test of Wilson's determination came over the

[2] Quoted in Charles E. Neu, *The Troubled Encounter: The United States and Japan* (New York, 1975), p. 99.

settlement of the Shantung issue. Should Japan be allowed to keep the former German concession? Wilson finally acquiesced, believing that Japan would otherwise refuse to join the League, and recognition of Japanese interests in Shantung was written into the Versailles Treaty.

Nonetheless, a new phase of East Asian international relations was opening, only in part because of America's shift in policy toward Japan's aspirations on the continent. Japan was confronted as well with increasing diplomatic coolness from another direction. Her special position in Korea and Manchuria had been protected under the imperialist system by agreements with Russia since 1905. But after 1917 the Soviet Union repudiated those agreements, owing to both ideological reasons growing out of Leninist doctrine on imperialism and strategic reasons that included closer Sino-Soviet relations. Perhaps even more ominous for the future, Japan now faced a rising tide of Asian nationalism in the form of anti-Japanese student demonstrations, which broke out on March 1, 1919 in Korea and on May 4, 1919 in Peking.

The Washington Treaty System

Hara and other perceptive Japanese leaders were acutely aware of such "new world trends" and came to feel that it was inevitable that Japan move in accord with them. They signaled their willingness to trim down Japan's continental aspirations, accept the disappearance of the former structure of imperialist diplomacy, and participate in a redefinition of mutual relations among the powers. A conference for this purpose was convened in Washington, at American initiative, in the autumn of 1921. American insistence led to the replacement of the expiring Anglo-Japanese Alliance by the innocuous Four Power Treaty, in which Britain, Japan, America, and France agreed to confer should the rights or possessions of any of the four in the Pacific be threatened. A Nine Power Treaty laid down the principles that were to guide the new order in East Asia: condemning spheres of influence in China, pledging equal opportunity for commerce and industry, and promising to respect the "sovereignty, the independence, and the territorial and administrative integrity of China." The conference sought to forestall a runaway naval arms race and to provide mutual security in the Five Power Naval Limitation Treaty, which restricted competition in battleships and aircraft carriers by setting a ratio of 5:5:3 for Britain, the United States, and Japan, respectively. The Japanese delegation believed this ratio of capital ships was sufficient to guarantee Japanese dominance in the western Pacific.

Japanese acceptance of the new framework of international relations was exemplified by the attitudes of Shidehara Kijurō, who was ambassador to Washington at the time of the Washington Conference and who was to serve as foreign minister (1924–1927 and 1929–1931). He shared the American vision of a liberal capitalist world order characterized by peace, political harmony, and economic interdependence. Cooperation with the United States was, after all, good business; the United States was Japan's largest supplier of capital and best trading customer, purchasing 40 percent of Japan's exports in the 1920s. Shidehara therefore advocated a posture of internationalism and peaceful development of Japan's overseas trade. Japan's policy, he held, should be to seek economic advancement in China and promotion of its own interests within the framework of international agreement. This willingness to abstain from aggressive pursuit of its political interests in China was, of course, pleasing to American policymakers. Franklin Roosevelt, who had earlier been among the sharp critics of Japan in the Navy Department, wrote in 1923 that the two nations "have not a single valid reason, and won't have as far as we can look ahead, for fighting each other."[3]

Yet there were many flaws marring the vision that Shidehara and the American policymakers shared. One appeared glaringly, the year after Roosevelt's statement, when Congress passed the Japanese Exclusion Act of 1924. Secretary of State Charles E. Hughes was "greatly depressed" by it and wrote that Congress "has undone the work of the Washington Conference and implanted the seeds of an antagonism which are sure to bear fruit in the future."[4] It made no difference that the Japanese themselves had been guilty of violent racism months earlier, in the massacre of thousands of Koreans after the earthquake; the Japanese press saw the new legislation as a national affront, and many writers interpreted it as further evidence of American perfidy.

Perhaps a more fundamental flaw in the new international vision was the failure of the high hopes held for economic expansionism. Partly, as we have seen, owing to the mistakes and indecisiveness of Japanese economic policymakers, foreign trade did not perform up to expectation. There were many obstacles. The United States followed a strongly protectionist course, and

[3] Quoted *ibid.*, p. 117.
[4] Quoted *ibid.*, p. 124.

Britain was making preferential tariff agreements within its empire that were detrimental to Japanese exports. In China, too, the nationalist movement demanded tariff autonomy and increasingly opposed Japanese economic interests. When to all these obstacles was added the onset of the Great Depression, the discontent and restlessness with Shidehara's internationalist diplomacy mounted. "It is a good thing to talk about economic foreign policy," said Matsuoka Yōsuke with sarcasm in the Diet in January 1931, "but we must have more than a slogan. Where are the fruits? We must be shown the benefit of this approach."[5] Matsuoka, who was to become foreign minister in 1940, believed that Shidehara's vision was bankrupt and that Japan must, by force if necessary, create its own economic bloc.

The most ominous threat to the Shidehara diplomacy was the challenge that the rising tide of nationalism in China represented for Japan's interests there. Shidehara worked with considerable skill to try to remove obstacles to the expansion of Japanese trade and investments in China, but history was hardly on his side. As China struggled painfully for institutional change and national unification, the question was insistently put to Japanese foreign policymakers: would Chinese nationalism cost Japan its special position in China? The Kuomintang, the Nationalist Party in China, embarked on its campaign of national unification, accompanied by radical antiforeign outbursts and by slogans demanding an end to the unequal treaties that the powers (including Japan) had forced China to sign. Beyond the problem of Japan's economic advancement was the still thornier question of Manchuria. If the Kuomintang campaign succeeded, could Japan preserve its treaty rights and interests in Manchuria? As this question was raised, Shidehara's "soft" policy of internationalism and support for the Washington treaty system began to rouse bitter resentment at home.

The Joining of Domestic and Foreign Crisis

In the years from 1928 to 1932 the ferment of political community at home was brought to crisis point by the onset of the depression and by the rising opposition to the framework of foreign relations established by the Washington Conference.

[5] Quoted in Akira Iriye, "The Failure of Economic Expansionism," in Bernard S. Silberman and Harry Harootunian (eds.), *Japan in Crisis* (Princeton, 1974), p. 265.

Resentment against the government's China policy was intense among leaders of the Kwantung Army, the unit of the Japanese army assigned to protect Japanese interests in Manchuria. They feared that without strong measures an opportunity to secure the Manchurian holdings would be lost. In 1928 as the Kuomintang armies moved closer to Peking and successful extension of Nationalist authority throughout North China, extremist elements in the Kwantung Army arranged the bombing of the train carrying Chang Tso-lin, the Manchurian warlord. Their expectation that this act would create disorder and give a pretext for expanded control of Manchuria failed to materialize, but the inability of Tokyo to punish the extremist elements in the army revealed not only the weakness of party government but also the potential for future insubordination.

Increasing tensions with China coincided with mounting discontent and unrest at home, as conservatives in and out of the government believed that Japan was besieged by radical thought. Following the general elections of 1928, the first in which the so-called proletarian parties participated, the nervous government on March 15, 1928 carried out a mass roundup of leftists. After sacking their headquarters, the government invoked the 1925 Peace Preservation Law to disband the Labor Farmer Party, the All-Japan Proletarian Youth Federation, and the Council of Japanese Labor Unions, which had fallen under the domination of the Communist Party. A year later the police arrested more than a thousand additional leftists in another lightning roundup.

The sense of crisis in society was further heightened by the collapse of the economy and the hardship it brought. From 1929 to 1931 exports fell by 50 percent, with disastrous effect on both city workers and farmers. In the cities unemployment rose and in the countryside, as the bottom fell out of commodity prices— especially silk and rice—real income was reduced by about one third from its 1925 levels. The government responded, as it had customarily to economic crises, by initiating another vigorous campaign of nationalist mobilization, on the one hand attacking leftist ideology as an un-Japanese importation from abroad and on the other hand exhorting still more intense loyalty to Japanese values and to the imperial symbol. In the past such campaigns had helped to dilute class consciousness and to undermine leftist social movements, but in this case the program contributed to an extremist patriotic movement, led by right-wing groups that proved difficult for even the government to control. Nervous bureaucrats, heretofore concerned with control of leftist groups, now found the secretive ultranationalist groups a bigger threat to social stability. It is a key to the events that followed to understand that decades of indoctrination, intended to overcome the social problems of industrialization by unifying the nation around traditional values of loyalty and solidarity, had created a populace highly receptive to the appeal of the most extreme nationalist slogans. In this time of social and economic crisis, when left-wing organizations were subject to intense scrutiny, radical right-wing groups came to exercise influence on restive elements in the army and in the civilian population.

Such an atmosphere made the party governments, which as we have seen had failed to develop a sense of legitimacy in the Japanese value system, particularly vulnerable to charges of failure and corruption. Above all, it made the maintenance of Shidehara's diplomacy, with its emphasis on internationalism and cooperation with the Anglo-American powers, increasingly difficult. The London Naval Conference of 1930, which was intended to extend the Washington treaty system, was particularly ill timed in the light of domestic developments in Japan. The prevailing 5:5:3 formula for capital ships was applied by the conference to heavy cruisers; and, in effect, a 10:10:7 formula for light cruisers was established for Britain, the United States, and Japan. Admirals in all three countries opposed the London treaty, but in the volatile atmosphere existing in Japan the opposition was explosive. Prime Minister Hamaguchi Osachi was charged with having compromised Japan's national security and with having trammeled the independent judgment of the naval command for the sake of a spurious friendship with the Anglo-American powers. On November 14, 1930, presaging an era of what a *New York Times* correspondent called "government by assassination," a young ultranationalist stepped from a crowd of well-wishers in Tokyo Station and shot the prime minister as he was preparing to board a train.

In the tense months that followed, Shidehara's hopes of establishing a new order in East Asia through cooperation with the United States and England were dashed by the determination in the Kwantung Army to resolve the Manchurian issue. It is surely true that the Anglo-American powers had not done enough to encourage and aid the hopeful effort of Shidehara, and by 1931 the opportunities for avoiding a collision between Japanese and Chinese nationalism were nearly gone. As one authority writes, "a strong government in Japan might have restrained army action in Manchuria and postponed a showdown with China on the basis of some compromise settlement on the issue of Japanese treaty rights. But the government in Tokyo was too weak and too unwilling to risk its existence by a strong stand." The government was subjected to increasing pressure from rival politicians and from the press to assert Japan's supremacy, and, on the Chinese side, Chiang Kai-shek was under pressure to adopt an inflexible attitude toward Japan. By the summer of 1931 "nothing short of the miraculous could prevent a clash in Manchuria."[6]

With the tacit consent of members of the General Staff, field grade officers of the Kwantung Army provoked an incident in Manchuria on the night of September 18, 1931. A small explosion on the tracks of the Japanese railway just north of Mukden was taken as sufficient pretext for mobilizing the Kwantung Army, attacking Chinese troops in the area, and expanding Japanese control. It was a critical moment for party government in Japan, although the response was in many ways foreordained by the nature and character the parties had formed as they rose to power. It was a moment when strong leadership and an appeal to traditions of responsible civilian government might have been effective, but the parties were accustomed to circumspection, compromise, and negotiation with the other elites. The Minseitō government of Wakatsuki Reijirō, who had succeeded Hamaguchi, temporized and attempted tactfully to limit the sphere of army action in Manchuria. But tact was ineffectual.

The weakness of the government, the diffuseness of decisionmaking power, the general confusion and uncertainty attending both domestic and foreign turmoil—all created an opportunity for resolute action by the Kwantung Army. It pushed ahead to conquer all of Manchuria and establish a Japanese puppet state, Manchukuo. Wakatsuki resigned and was replaced by a Seiyūkai cabinet headed by Inukai Tsuyoshi. It was the last party government in prewar Japan. The efforts of the aging Inukai to restore order were ill starred. His own party's Diet members voted to withdraw from the League of Nations, should that body censure Japan's action in Manchuria. Ultranationalism as a popular phenomenon now gained sway. Fanatic groups, committed to cleansing the body politic by replacing the political and economic elites and carrying out a "restoration," assassinated the former finance minister in February 1932, then the chief director of the Mitsui zaibatsu in March, and finally Inukai himself on May 15.

[6] Akira Iriye, *After Imperialism: The Search for a New Order in the Far East 1931–1933* (Cambridge, Mass., 1965), pp. 295–296.

Going It Alone

After decades of sowing the winds of nationalism among the Japanese people, the elites were now reaping the whirlwind. They had used education, the media, and a variety of grassroots organizations to mobilize nationalist sentiment among the populace for the hard struggles required to support industrialism and imperialism, and now the government was caught in a trap of its own making. Popular nationalism became a runaway force, extremely difficult to control—especially where government was so weak and so cumbersome. This nationalism was particularly unruly among leaders of society at the local level—the elementary school principal, the Shinto priest in the village, the mayor and headman of the community, the head of the local chapter of the military association, and the like. That stratum of lower middle-class leadership, which had climbed only halfway up the ladder of success, was the group toward which government mobilization efforts had been particularly directed. Such local leaders had been exhorted to interpret Japan's mission to the masses, and charged with responsibility for fulfilling Japan's destiny. As "true believers" in the collectivist ethic, they were the most impatient with the cosmopolitanism of the business elite and the squabbles and corruption of party politicians. Ultranationalist groups seeking radical solutions to the nation's problems could count on their support.

Nationalism gripped every part of Japanese society. Even the Communists—in overwhelming numbers—underwent swift conversions in prison in the early 1930s, renouncing their earlier theories and in many cases joining enthusiastically in the rhetoric of nationalism. Leaders of the ultranationalist groups set the tone of Japanese politics in the ensuing several years. Following Inukai's assassination, the one remaining genrō, Saionji Kimmochi, turned to moderate elements in the military to lead in the formation of cabinets, hoping that they could succeed where party politicians had failed in controlling the extremist elements in the army. For the next four years, from 1932 through 1936, the country was governed by cabinets twice headed by admirals. It was no easy matter to maintain moderate policies in the face of mounting ultranationalist sympathies, which were fueled by a growing sense of isolation as the seizure of Manchuria drew international condemnation. When the League of Nations adopted the Lytton Commission's report condemning Japan as an aggressor, the Japanese delegation walked out of the hall and out of the League.

The Manchurian Incident thus proved a turning point—a

point at which Japan abandoned the general policy of cooperation with the powers, which had for the most part controlled its
international behavior since 1868, and chose to pursue its own
destiny in East Asia, to trust its own strength to protect and
advance its interests. The leadership now spoke of an "Asian
Monroe Doctrine," declaring Japan's responsibility for maintaining peace in Asia. In thus choosing to abandon its customary
circumspection, and to withdraw from the Washington treaty
system, Japan set formidable requirements for the nation's defense. To maintain the strategic posture demanded by its "Monroe Doctrine" and by the commitment to Manchukuo, Japan
now needed military power sufficient for three major tasks: to
defeat the Soviet army, whose strength on the borders of Manchuria had been vastly augmented; to guarantee the security of
the home islands against the American fleet; and to compel the
Chinese government to accept Japan's position in Manchuria
and northern China.

These three strategic objectives required a military capabil-
ity that Japan was never able to achieve. The Meiji oligarchs
would have been appalled at the incautious way in which policy
commitments were made that exceeded the nation's capacities.
How was it that Japan's leaders in the early 1930s embarked on
so perilous a course? In part, the answer lies in the fragmented
nature of decisionmaking in the Japanese government, which at
that time lacked a strong, central controlling leadership able to
exercise its will over all factions of the administration, and able
to coordinate and develop prudent and balanced policy goals. In
part, too, it lies in the combination of ambition for Asian leadership and frustration with the Washington treaty system and
with events in China. Moreover, leaders in the early 1930s were
making policy in an atmosphere often dominated by the ultranationalist sentiment that, although they may not have
sympathized with it, subtly affected and conditioned their thinking.

Initially the reorientation of national policy seemed to be a
success. In spite of the League's condemnation, Manchuria was
now secure to be developed and integrated into the Japanese
industrial machine. Moreover, in the years after the Manchurian
takeover, Japanese economic policy scored phenomenal success
in achieving rapid recovery from the depression. Hugh Patrick
calls it "one of the most successful combinations of fiscal, mone-
tary, and foreign exchange rate policies, in an adverse international environment, that the world has ever seen."[7] To a con-

[7] Patrick in James W. Morley (ed.), *Dilemmas of Growth in Prewar Japan*
(Princeton, 1971), p. 256.

siderable extent it was a matter of good luck. In the aftermath of Manchuria, the government was required by the new international conditions to begin a rapid buildup of its industrial and military plant. Over the next two years the government increased expenditures by 26 percent, under a great deal of pressure not to raise taxes. Therefore the increased government spending was deficit financed, and as a result greatly enlarged private demand and consequently stimulated the economy. Most of the increase in government spending during the 1930s was, of course, for military purposes, but all sectors of the economy benefited. Japan gave up the gold standard in December 1931, and this proved a boon for Japanese exports. Overall, the growth rate of the real net domestic product during the 1930s was more than double that of the previous decade. Economic growth however did not, as it sometimes does, moderate policy. If anything, it seemed to confirm the new course.

In the five years after the seizure of Manchuria violence and ultranationalist sentiment continued very much a part of the domestic political scene. Rival cliques vied for ascendancy in the army, resorting to assassination of one of the top generals in 1935, and culminating the next year in an all-out insurrection. On February 26, 1936, fourteen hundred soldiers from the First Division in Tokyo, led by young officers plotting a radical reconstruction of the government, rebelled. They seized control of the Diet and the main army and government offices and murdered the finance minister, the lord keeper of the privy seal, and the inspector general of military education. The prime minister, the last of the genrō, Saionji, and other leaders narrowly escaped. With the Emperor's backing, the rival faction subdued the young officers' insurrection and disposed of its leaders, but the net result was to leave the government even more clearly in the grip of the military. Discipline was re-established, but the range of political debate was still further narrowed and ultranationalist sentiment heightened.

The Coming of the Pacific War

In the summer of 1937 Japan blundered into war with China. It was not a war that the Army General Staff wanted, but having chosen to abandon the principles of the Washington treaty system, and operating in an atmosphere dominated by ultranationalist goals and a growing willingness to resort to military solutions, the government was ill prepared to restrain itself. In June 1937 Konoe Fumimaro was chosen by Saionji to become

Schoolgirls in celebration at the Imperial Palace after the fall of Nanking in December 1937. *National Archives*

prime minister. Prince Konoe was a widely respected figure from an old noble family, who might, it was thought, succeed in uniting the country and restraining the military. He spoke of achieving "social justice" in domestic affairs, but he proved a weak and ineffectual leader. It was during his first tenure as prime minister (June 1937–January 1939) that the nation stumbled into full-scale war with China, and during his second tenure (July 1940–October 1941) that fateful steps were taken toward Pearl Harbor.

Since 1931 there had been general consensus that if new conflict came, it would likely be with the Soviet Union. A prime goal of the general staff, therefore, was to concentrate on the economic development of Manchukuo and its integration into the industrial complex of Japan so as to increase the strength of the military establishment. Conflict with the Nationalist government in China was, therefore, to be avoided as a hindrance to the implementation of the plans designed to prepare for war with Russia. The General Staff in the spring of 1937 had, in fact, ordered Japanese commanders of military forces in north China to avoid incidents that might disrupt the status quo. When a minor skirmish broke out on July 7, 1937 between Chinese and Japanese troops stationed in the Marco Polo Bridge area, just outside of Peking, the Japanese army sought to achieve a quick local settlement. But the incident could not be so easily contained; instead it swiftly escalated into full-scale hostilities. Chiang Kai-shek, the Nationalist leader, under immense pressure to resist Japanese encroachment, was doubtless determined not to allow any new pretext like the Mukden Incident of 1931 to serve the Japanese expansionist cause. He therefore responded to the Marco Polo Bridge Incident by dispatching four divisions to north China. Konoe responded with an ill-advised sword-rattling statement, which only served to confirm Chiang in his suspicions, and hopes of attaining a local settlement evaporated.

It is not easy, even in retrospect, to see how conflict between China and Japan could have been avoided. History sometimes brings nations into logjams from which they are extricated only by force. Chinese nationalism could no longer tolerate the status quo with Japan. Yet Japanese of all persuasions looked at Japan's position in China as sanctioned by economic need and by their destiny to create "a new order in Asia" that would expel Western influence and establish a structure based upon Asian concepts of justice and humanity. Chiang's government was regarded as an obstruction that had to be overcome on the way to this "new order," and so in 1938 Konoe called for an all-out campaign to "annihilate" the Nationalist regime. The expectation was that Chinese resistance would be short-lived: a "fundamental resolution of Sino-Japanese relations" could be achieved by compelling the Nationalists to accept Japanese leadership in creating an Asian community of nations, free of Anglo-American capitalism and Soviet Communism. It was a fateful decision. It tragically underrated the difficulties involved, not least the strength of Chinese nationalism; it brought totalitarian controls at home and vastly heightened tensions with the United States. But Japanese leadership pushed ahead with supreme nerve justifying their goals with Pan-Asian slogans and, ultimately, with the vision of a Greater East Asia Coprosperity Sphere from which all vestiges of Western imperialism would be erased.

The dilemma that Japanese diplomacy had struggled with ever since the Manchurian Incident now became still more difficult, for as the China conflict expanded, the nation was the less prepared to deal with the Soviet army on the Manchurian border and the American fleet in the Pacific. A succession of border skirmishes with the Red Army revealed the vulnerability of the Kwantung Army; at the same time the American navy was now embarked on a resolute program of building additional strength in the Pacific. By the spring of 1940 the Japanese Navy General Staff had concluded that America's crash program would result in its gaining naval hegemony in the Pacific by 1942, and that Japan must have access to the oil of the Dutch East Indies in order to cope with American power. Konoe's impulsive and unstable foreign minister, Matsuoka Yōsuke, set out to resolve the impasse by a swift demarche. In the autumn of 1940 he signed the Tripartite Pact with Germany and Italy, in which the signatories pledged to aid one another if attacked by a power not currently involved in the European war or the fighting in China. Matsuoka thereby hoped to isolate the United States and dissuade it from conflict with Japan, thus opening the way for Japan to seize the European colonies in Southeast Asia, grasp the resources it needed for self-sufficiency, and cut off Chinese supply lines. Furthermore, to free his northern flank he signed a neutrality pact with the USSR in April 1941; and when Hitler attacked Russia in June the Manchukuo-Soviet border seemed wholly secure. Within weeks Japanese troops entered Indochina.

American reaction to the Tripartite Pact was, to Matsuoka, unexpectedly strong. President Franklin D. Roosevelt forbade any further shipment of scrap iron to Japan, and after the entry into Indochina he embargoed oil. Negotiations between Secretary of State Cordell Hull and Ambassador Nomura Kichisaburō foundered in a morass of confusion and ineptness. It is doubtful that negotiations had much opportuniy for success in any case at this juncture—given the positions taken by the two sides. Hull's insistence on Japanese withdrawal from China was seen as nullifying a decade of foreign policy and reducing Japan to a second-class power.

Rather than turn back, Japanese leaders were prepared to take risks. "Nothing ventured, nothing gained," Matsuoka concluded. "We should take decisive action."[8] And the new prime minister, General Tōjō Hideki, was quoted as saying, "Sometimes people have to shut their eyes and take the plunge."[9] The Navy General Staff in particular pressed for war, arguing that oil reserves were limited and American naval strength increasing. Ultimately its reasoning was accepted, and the president of the Privy Council explained to the Emperor a month before Pearl Harbor, "It is impossible from the standpoint of our domestic political situation and of our self-preservation, to accept all of the American demands. . . . If we miss the present opportunity to go to war, we will have to submit to American dictation. Therefore, I recognize that it is inevitable that we must decide to start a war against the United States. I will put my

[8] Quoted in Jansen, *Japan and China*, p. 404.
[9] Quoted in Masao Maruyama, *Thought and Behaviour in Modern Japanese Politics* (Oxford, 1969; rev. ed.), p. 85.

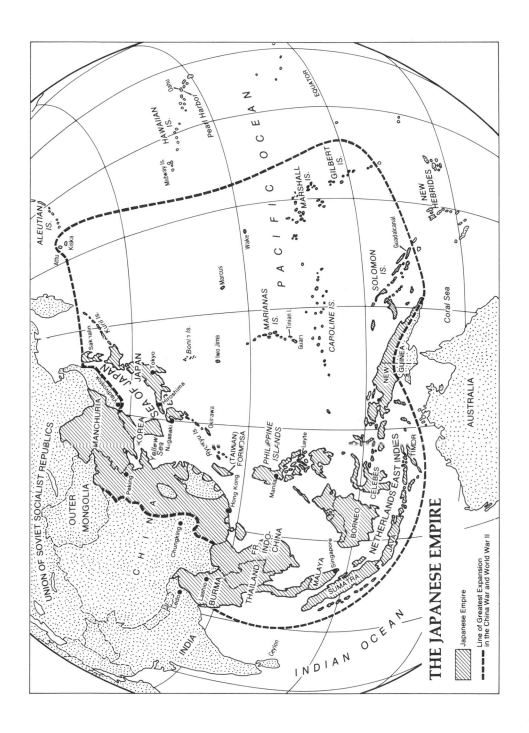

THE JAPANESE EMPIRE

⬚ Japanese Empire

▬ ▬ Line of Greatest Expansion
in the China War and World War II

149

trust in what I have been told: namely, that things will go well in the early part of the war; and that although we will experience increasing difficulties as the war progresses, there is some prospect of success."[10]

Japan paid a terrible price for the bold gamble of its leaders in 1941. Abandoning the cautious realism that had traditionally characterized Japanese diplomacy, the nation entered into a conflict that cost it its entire overseas empire; the destruction of a quarter of its machines, equipment, buildings, and houses; and the lives of nearly three million Japanese. Generations were left physically and psychologically scarred by the trauma.

The outcome was heavy with historical irony. War sentiment in Japan had been impelled by an ultranationalist ideology that sought to preserve the traditional values of the Japanese political order, that vehemently opposed the expansion of Bolshevik influence in Asia, and that wanted to establish the Japanese empire. Instead, war brought a social-democratic revolution at home, the rise of Communism in China, and—for the first time in its history—occupation by an enemy force.

[10] Quoted in Jansen, *Japan and China*, p. 405.

In the weeks and months after Pearl Harbor the Japanese Empire was aggrandized by success after success. The British naval base at Singapore was seized in February 1942, and the following month the entire Dutch East Indies was in Japanese hands; by April Japanese forces controlled a major part of the Philippines and by May they had penetrated far into the northern reaches of Burma, where they could cut off the supplies flowing into China.

At home a new feeling of destiny was in the air. After years of inconclusive fighting in China, there was a broadly expressed sense of joy and relief that total war had been declared. A distinguished novelist and critic, Itō Sei, wrote that on first hearing of the declaration of war, "I felt as if in one stroke I had become a new man, from the depths of my being." He went on:

This war is an absolute act. It is not merely an extension of politics or the reverse side of politics. It is a struggle which the [Japanese] people had some day to fight in order to convince themselves from the bottom of their hearts that they are the most excellent people on the face of the globe. We are the "yellow race" our enemies talk about. We are fighting to determine the superiority or inferiority of the discriminated-against peoples. Our struggle is not the same as Germany's. . . .[1]

But as the president of the Privy Council had forecast to the Emperor on the eve of Pearl Harbor, Japan experienced growing difficulties as the war continued. By mid-1942, following the battles of the Coral Sea and Midway, Japanese forces were on the defensive. In most of the countries that the Japanese entered, the ideology of pan-Asianism and of the Coprosperity Sphere had little staying power. At home, the government required

JAPAN'S AMERICAN REVOLUTION

12

[1] Quoted in Donald Keene, *Landscapes and Portraits: Appreciations of Japanese Culture* (Tokyo, 1971), p. 303.

greater and greater sacrifices from the Japanese people. The portion of the gross national product devoted to the war effort increased from 31 percent in 1942 to 42 percent in 1943 and then to 51 percent in 1944. American ships dominated the Pacific and cut off the import of raw materials. Agricultural production was curtailed by the shortage of chemical fertilizers and by the loss of farm labor to war-related industries. American fire-bomb raids brought terrible suffering to the already under-nourished and disease-prone urban population. An incendiary raid on Tokyo, March 10, 1945 killed over 100,000 people. Cities across the country were laid waste through thousands of sorties by American bombers, often flying at chimney-top level. By mid-summer 1945 the Japanese were a weary and demoralized people, living in silent desperation and resigned to defeat.

In July 1945 the leaders of Great Britain, Russia, and the United States met at Potsdam and issued a declaration that warned Japan to surrender or face "prompt and utter destruction." President Harry S Truman learned of the successful testing of an atomic device during the conference and therefore felt confident in demanding unconditional surrender. The Potsdam Declaration listed the Allies' objectives of dismantling the Japanese Empire and establishing a democratic order, but, partly because it did not clarify what would happen to the imperial institution, the Japanese government rejected the declaration on July 28. Accordingly, the atomic bomb was used on Hiroshima on August 6, killing, by Japanese estimates, 87,150; and three days later almost as many died in the atomic bombing of Nagasaki.

In the wake of these events and of the entrance of the Soviet Union into the war, an imperial conference was convened at which the Emperor personally intervened to express his will that the Allied demands be accepted. On August 15 he broadcast an Imperial Rescript enjoining the Japanese people to bear the unbearable and to surrender with decorum. The broadcast was met with an emotional combination of relief and anguish: the war was over, but Japan was to be occupied by enemy soldiers for the first time in its history.

The American Occupation

Although nominally the Allies occupied Japan, in fact the enterprise was overwhelmingly American. It was dominated by the personality of General Douglas MacArthur, who was appointed

Supreme Commander of the Allied Powers (SCAP). Though he received broad policy directives from Washington, MacArthur was given broad discretion in the implementation of reforms, and his personal dominance was so great that the term "SCAP" soon came to designate the entire occupation administration. Unlike Germany, where collapse of the wartime government compelled the occupying forces to assume direct control, Japan had a government still intact at the time of surrender, and so SCAP was able to govern indirectly as a supervisory organ above the existing government.

From the beginning, two fundamental beliefs underlay United States planning for the occupation. In the first place, there was an insistent faith in the universality of American values and institutions. Those enduring results of the American experience, MacArthur wrote in 1947, "are no longer peculiarly American, but now belong to the entire human race." It was believed that the United States, with all its faults, was the most advanced of all nations; and since all societies had to develop along more or less the same lines, reforms in Japanese society should be modeled along American lines. Japan therefore became the subject of an extraordinary experiment in the transference of American ideals and institutions to an Asian setting.

The other fundamental tenet in the philosophy of the occupation was the belief that the most effective way of curing the Japanese of their militarism was by creating a democratic society. If people were given control of their own destiny, they would by nature and out of self-interest choose a peaceful course. "War's genesis," wrote the Supreme Commander, "lies in the despotic lust for power. . . . Never has it originated in the voluntary action of a free people—never will a free people voluntarily associate itself with the proposition that the road to peace and well-being and happiness lies through the crucible of war."[2] Those two fundamental beliefs moved the Americans to undertake the most radical reforms ever made in Japanese society.

The reforms could not successfully have been imposed had there not been a warm receptivity to undertaking such changes. Many Japanese felt that their prewar leaders had led them astray and that sweeping reform of Japanese institutions was necessary. They often referred to the occupation as the "second opening of Japan," similar to the period nearly a century earlier when the country had received new and rejuvenating influences

[2] *Life* (magazine), July 4, 1947.

from the outside. For the Japanese, the occupation period was a time of intense self-criticism and introspection, of revulsion for much that was old and traditional. This mood fed on itself and created a disposition in favor of innovation. As a consequence, reform became the vogue and the occupation's task was greatly facilitated.

Demilitarization

The initial task the Americans set for themselves was to destroy the military system that had been built up since the Meiji Restoration. That entailed disbanding the military and secret police forces and closing bases, arsenals, and munitions factories; it also meant punishing or dismissing the leaders held responsible for the system, and discrediting the values they had sponsored. Only after the field was cleared in this fashion, it was believed, could democratic institutions be successfully implanted.

The months after surrender brought a confusing relocation of vast numbers of weary and uncertain people. Over five million troops, more than half of whom were overseas, had to be demobilized and disarmed. In addition, over three million civil-

Defeated Japanese soldiers sit on Tokyo sidewalks waiting for demobilization, September 1945. *National Archives*

ians who had held positions in Japanese overseas territories streamed back into the home islands, placing still more stress on the debilitated economy. Factories that had produced for the military were closed, their employees turned out, and machinery was shipped off to neighboring countries as part of a reparations policy.

One of the most controversial aspects of the occupation was the International Military Tribunal for the Far East, which MacArthur created to try war criminals. The trials of the Japanese leaders dragged on for over two years, and eventually seven men, including former Prime Ministers Tōjō and Hirota Kōki, were sentenced to death by hanging. Sixteen leaders were sentenced to prison for life, one for twenty years, and former Foreign Minister Shigemitsu for seven years. The issues raised by these convictions, such as the principle of holding individual leaders responsible for acts of their government, and subjecting them to alien, ex post facto laws, have been the subject of continuing controversy. In addition to this retribution, hundreds of lower-ranking officers were executed for atrocities and thousands of others sentenced to various terms of imprisonment.

The determination of SCAP to revolutionize Japanese society was made clear right at the outset by a decision to remove nearly the entire stratum of prewar leadership. A "purge" directive was issued on January 4, 1946, which automatically removed from eligibility for political office anyone who had played a part in promoting "Japanese aggression or militant nationalism." Military officers, heads of overseas business organizations, colonial officers, and leaders of nationalist organizations were purged. In all, 220,000 persons were declared ineligible to hold office in the new political order. One prominent American writer visiting Japan was stunned by the policy: "This use of the word 'purge' was new to me; I had never heard it in political talk except in connection with Russia."[3] But SCAP felt no self-doubts, in the belief that if the former oppressive forces were swept clear then democratic forces would naturally grow up and flourish. The purge was executed swiftly and mechanically with little time allowed for reviewing individual cases. A serious shortcoming in the policy was the exemption of the civilian bureaucracy from the purge. With some exceptions, SCAP left the bureaucracy intact, for it was needed to run the day-to-day business of government. As a consequence, the bureaucracy preserved remarkable strength of continuity from prewar days

[3] John Gunther, *The Riddle of MacArthur* (New York, 1951), p. 149.

and became the major power in postwar politics—to the detriment of democratic forces.

A New Political Order

Once these measures—demobilizing the armed forces, destroying war-related industries, purging the prewar leadership, and trying war criminals—were accomplished, the occupation was ready to turn to the creative tasks of building a new democratic order. The tone was set by proclaiming a "Japanese Bill of Rights," which abolished all restrictions on speech and assembly and threw open the gates to free about 2,500 political prisoners, many of whom were Communists. SCAP later regretted this enthusiasm, but the measure reveals the high idealism of the early occupation days.

The thorniest problem MacArthur and his staff had to deal with was deciding the fate of the Emperor. In most of the Allied countries there was strong sentiment in favor of destroying the imperial institution and trying Hirohito as a war criminal. Months went by after surrender without any firm decision by the American government. MacArthur himself was impressed with the Emperor at their first meeting, and the photograph of the two men taken at the time records one of the most poignant moments in Japanese history: the Supreme Commander, casual in his fatigues, hands on hips, towering over the nervous Son of Heaven, standing at attention in formal attire.

The Emperor's advisors worked shrewdly to try to change his image. It was their idea, apparently, that he make a formal renunciation of his "sacred and inviolable" status. On New Year's Day 1946, Hirohito made his so-called Declaration of Humanity, in which he stated that "the ties between Us and Our people . . . do not depend upon mere legends and myths. They are not predicated on the false conception that the Emperor is divine, and that the Japanese people are superior to other races and fated to rule the world."

MacArthur came to the conclusion that the imperial institution was necessary to maintain political stability and to sanction and facilitate reform. He wanted the Emperor kept as a constitutional monarch and therefore sought to convince Washington by predicting catastrophic consequences if the Emperor were removed: "The whole of Japan can be expected, in my opinion, to resist. . . . I believe all hope of introducing modern democratic methods would disappear. . . . It is quite possible that a minimum of a million troops would be required which

The first meeting of General MacArthur and the Emperor. *Courtesy of International Society for Educational Information, Tokyo, Inc.*

would have to be maintained for an indefinite number of years. In addition a complete civil service might have to be recruited and imported, possibly running into a size of several hundred thousand."[4] In the face of such determined advice the opposition in Washington withered, and the decision was made to preserve the imperial institution as the symbolic head of a new democratic state.

[4] United States Department of State, *Foreign Relations of the United States: 1946* (Washington, 1971), VIII, pp. 395–396.

Scarcely less vexing was the problem of constitutional revision. There was general agreement among American planners that the Meiji Constitution would have to be wholly rewritten. It was seen as having blocked the development of democratic politics and as being partly responsible for the growth of militarism. Still, the hope in Washington was that SCAP could maintain a low profile and allow the Japanese themselves to conduct the process of revision, lest knowledge that constitutional reforms had been imposed reduce the possibility of their acceptance and support by the Japanese people in the future. Therefore, MacArthur asked the new prime minister, Shidehara —SCAP had some confidence in him because of his liberal foreign policy during the 1920s—to undertake "liberalization of the constitution." The latter appointed a distinguished committee of legal scholars and bureaucrats for this purpose, and for three months the committee deliberated. On February 1, 1946, the proposals of the committee were presented to MacArthur.

They proved, however, to be highly conservative, amounting only to limited revisions of the Meiji Constitution. At this point MacArthur decided to intrude upon the constitutional revision. He clearly felt that if left to the Japanese the process would be too slow and painful. He wanted to get on with creation of a new political order, and nothing could be done until the basic document was written. MacArthur therefore pushed ahead and proceeded, behind the scenes, to impose his own version of a constitution. He ordered the Government Section of SCAP to draft a constitution that could serve as a "guide" for the Japanese cabinet. The head of the Government Section, General Courtney Whitney, was instructed that the document should provide for the Emperor as a constitutional monarch, "responsible to an electorate based upon wide representative suffrage," and should declare that "war and war-making would be forsworn."

So far as we know, the decision to insert a clause in the constitution renouncing war and a standing army grew out of a conversation that Shidehara and MacArthur had on January 24, 1946. In his *Reminiscences* the latter writes that Shidehara suggested to him that the constitution "prohibit any military establishment" so that "the rest of the world would know that Japan never intended to wage war again." This suggestion may well have come as part of the Japanese effort to improve the negative image of the Emperor. MacArthur writes that when he agreed with the suggestion, Shidehara's "amazement was so great that he seemed overwhelmed as he left the office. Tears ran down his face, and he turned back to me and said, 'the world will laugh and mock us as impracticable visionaries, but a hundred years from now we will be called prophets.' "[5]

In an almost Alice-in-Wonderland atmosphere Whitney assembled members of his Government Section, proclaimed them "a constitutional assembly," and directed them to draft a document. In six days (!) the task was complete, the product handed to MacArthur for his approval, and on February 13, 1946, it was presented to the Japanese cabinet at a meeting in the foreign minister's residence. The cabinet members were put under heavy pressure, with the implied threat to go directly to the Japanese people if the document were not accepted. On March 5 the cabinet, after making some minor changes, approved the MacArthur draft and passed it on to the Emperor, who dutifully accepted it. The following day it was made public, and MacArthur gave a poker-faced statement to the press praising the Japanese for "such an exemplary document which so coincided with his own notion of what was best for the country." It was unlikely that many were misled to believe this was a Japanese product, for the language and concepts were patched together from the Anglo-American political tradition and had unmistakable echoes of the Declaration of Independence, the Constitution of the United States, and the Gettysburg Address.

The new constitution made a number of revolutionary changes in the Japanese political order:

1. It reduced the Emperor, formerly sacred and inviolable, to a position as "the symbol of the State and of the unity of the people with whom resides sovereign power."

2. It provided that "the Japanese people forever renounce war as a sovereign right" and declared that "land, sea, and air forces, as well as other war potential, will never be maintained" (Article 9).

3. It made the cabinet responsible to the Diet, as in the British system; and it made the legislature, which under the Meiji Constitution had been partly elective by male suffrage and partly appointive, entirely elective by universal suffrage.

4. It replaced the highly centralized structure of government under the Meiji system with one that allowed a much greater measure of local autonomy, by increasing the power of local officials and making their positions elective.

5. It created an independent judiciary with the right of judicial review.

[5] Excerpted from *Reminiscences* by Douglas MacArthur, McGraw-Hill, copyright © 1964 by Time, Inc., p. 303.

6. It afforded protection for a wide variety of human rights: freedom of the press, freedom of assembly, academic freedom, equality of the sexes, and collective bargaining.

Economic Reforms

SCAP set out similarly to democratize the economy. Washington had ordered MacArthur to reform labor, business, and agriculture so as to accomplish "a wide distribution of income and of the ownership of the means of production." Occupation planners blamed the prewar concentration of economic power in the hands of the big business and landlord classes for creating the social environment in which militarism could take root. Moreover, since many of the planners had earlier worked for the New Deal programs of Franklin Roosevelt, they were predisposed in favor of economic reform that would alleviate the frustrations of industrial workers and tenant farmers.

The influence of the New Deal was particularly apparent in the reforms undertaken to promote the labor union movement and to break up the giant industrial combines. SCAP prodded the Diet to pass a trade union act in December 1945, which was patterned after the Wagner Act passed by the United States Congress ten years earlier. This "Magna Carta of Japanese Labor" guaranteed the rights of workers to organize, to bargain collectively, and to strike; and it prohibited various unfair practices by employers. Subsequent legislation provided for minimum working conditions, unemployment insurance, and procedures for resolution of labor disputes.

The occupation enthusiastically promoted campaigns of unionization, and the number of members grew rapidly. During the prewar period only 420,000 of a total industrial labor force of six million workers were union members, in the peak year of membership. By June 1948, thanks to the prodding of SCAP, union membership soared to six and a half million members. Yet the significance of this figure may be easily exaggerated, for the values underlying the union movement in Western democracies were frequently absent from a movement brought into being more by government initiative than by the voluntary action of laboring men and women themselves. It was not uncommon for the head of a firm to take the initiative in organizing a union in his own company.

Much controversy was generated by the occupation's program to break up the zaibatsu, those vast economic combines such as Mitsui, Mitsubishi, Sumitomo, and Yasuda. Products of Japanese economic growth and of the need to concentrate capital, skilled labor, and technology, they were seen by the Americans as obstacles to economic democracy. An economics professor who had participated in antitrust actions during the New Deal and who was brought to Tokyo to advise the occupation wrote that "concentration of economic control enabled [the zaibatsu] to continue a semi-feudal relationship between themselves and their employees, to continue to suppress wages and to hinder the development of independent political ideologies. Thus the formation of the middle class, which was useful in opposing the militarist group in other democratic countries, was retarded."[6]

To bring about a deconcentration of economic power, the occupation dissolved 10 holding companies as well as the 26 largest industrial companies and the 2 largest trading companies. In addition, a "shareholding revolution" was carried out, which sought to diffuse the stocks of over 600 companies into the hands of many. In less than two years nearly 1.4 million shares were sold to the public. In April 1947 the Diet was prodded into passage of legislation modeled on American antitrust laws, which established a Fair Trade Commission to police business and to prohibit monopoly practice.

The most successful of the economic measures engineered by the Americans was the program of land reform. It was an idea that captured MacArthur's imagination, perhaps because of Jeffersonian ideas that survived from his early days in Virginia —or perhaps because of his father's participation in land reform in the Philippines at the turn of the century. In any case, SCAP pressured the Japanese government into a far-reaching program that called for a complete dispossession of absentee landlords and for retention by other owners of up to 7.5 acres farmed by the owner himself and of an additional 2.5 acres more of tenanted land. (Somewhat larger plots were permitted in Hokkaido.) The government purchased all land in excess of these limits and sold it to the existing tenants on easy terms. The reform was an immense undertaking, involving the establishment of over 11,000 local land commissions, which were composed of tenants and owners and which instituted changes in the property rights of some six million families and hence in the whole fabric of social relations. The amount of land under tenancy agreement was reduced from over 40 percent to around 10 percent, transforming the countryside into a society of small independent farmers.

[6] Corwin Edwards quoted in Kozo Yamamura, *Economic Policy in Postwar Japan* (Berkeley, 1967), p. 2.

Social Reforms

MacArthur and many of the American policy planners believed that the fundamental success of the occupation reforms would depend upon a transformation of society and its supporting values, which they believed were still basically feudal. "Supposedly," MacArthur wrote, "the Japanese were a twentieth-century civilization. In reality, they were more nearly a feudal society, of the type discarded by Western nations some four centuries ago."[7] The occupation therefore set about liberalizing the entire social structure and converting Japan to a philosophy of democratic individualism.

The Americans took special pride in bringing about what they regarded as "the emancipation of the women in Japan." Female suffrage was one of their primary goals, and when the first general elections of the postwar period were held in April 1946, over thirteen million women voted for the first time and thirty-eight women were elected to the Diet. Recalling this election, MacArthur writes in his *Reminiscences* that a distraught Japanese legislative leader visited him after the returns were in and reported:

> "I regret to say that something terrible has happened. A prostitute, Your Excellency, has been elected to the House of Representatives."
>
> I asked him, "How many votes did she receive?"
>
> The Japanese legislator sighed and said: "256,000."
>
> I said as solemnly as I could: "Then I should say there must have been more than her dubious occupation involved."
>
> He burst into a gale of laughter. "You soldiers!" he exclaimed and dropped the subject. He probably thought I was a lunatic.[8]

The constitution explicitly provided that "equality of the sexes" should govern matters of property rights and inheritance, and it stated that "marriage shall be based only on the mutual consent of both sexes and it shall be maintained through mutual cooperation with the equal rights of husband and wife as a basis." These principles were incorporated into a new Civil Code, which came into effect on January 1, 1948.

Another important part of SCAP's effort to transform Japanese society and its supporting values was the reform of the education system. The United States Education Mission, a

---

[7] Excerpted from *Reminiscences* by Douglas MacArthur, McGraw-Hill, copyright © 1964 by Time, Inc., p. 283.
[8] *Ibid.*, p. 305.

twenty-seven-member group of educators that made a whirl-wind tour of Japan in the spring of 1946, recommended what proved tantamount to wholesale adoption of the American education system and its philosophy. One of the first tasks recommended by the mission was to carry out a vast decentralization of the functions of the heretofore powerful Ministry of Education. The ministry's tight control over secondary education was to be superseded by popularly elected boards of education at the local level, which were given control of staff, curriculum, and choosing textbooks. Other structural reforms imitated the American pattern. In place of the former multitrack educational system, which SCAP considered undemocratic and elitist, it established a single-track coeducational plan along American lines, with six years of elementary schooling, followed by three years of junior high school and three years of senior high school for all children. Similarly, at the postsecondary level the old differentiation among technical schools, normal schools, and imperial universities was done away with, and all institutions of higher learning were reorganized as four-year universities. Many critics have argued that, as a consequence, Japanese education became homogenized in a way that diluted the strengths of the old differentiated and diverse system.

SCAP's educational reformers also wanted to root out the nationalist orientation of the schools and replace it with a strong democratic and individualist philosophy. The Diet rescinded the Imperial Rescript on Education, which had been in effect since 1890 and which had set the nationalist tone of educational values. In its place, the Fundamental Law of Education of 1947 defined the purpose of the education system as contributing to "the peace of the world and the welfare of humanity by building a democratic and cultural state." As is always the case after a revolution, history had to be rewritten; in this instance new textbooks emphasized the themes of peace, democracy, and international cooperation. Also, as the teachers became organized into a powerful trade union dominated by left-wing politics, most history texts stressed such concepts as economic exploitation and the struggle of the people against the oppression of the ruling class. As a result, the education system became deeply enmeshed in partisan politics in the postwar era.

The "Reverse Course"

Occupation policy comprised two main phases. During the first two years, from 1945 to 1947, under the sway of postwar ideals that sought elimination of militarism and establishment of a democratic society, Americans consciously played the role of revolutionary. By 1947 there was a feeling within SCAP that the work of reform was nearly complete, and MacArthur, at a press conference in March, surprised reporters by suggesting that it was time to plan the end of the occupation. But before his hopes could materialize, the onset of the Cold War began to transform the outlook and approach of policy planners. By 1948 the tension between the Soviet Union and the United States and the growing power of the Chinese Communist movement led the U.S. State Department to rethink American objectives for Japan. George Kennan, the new director of the State Department's Policy Planning Staff, recommended after a trip to Tokyo that "no further reform legislation should be pressed. The emphasis should shift from reform to economic recovery. . . . precedence should be given . . . to the task of bringing the Japanese into a position where they would be better able to shoulder the burdens of independence."[9]

Accordingly, a marked shift in occupation policy ensued, one that many dismayed Japanese intellectuals and writers subsequently termed "the reverse course." It seemed to them that Americans were going back on the principles and programs enunciated during the preceding two years. To a considerable extent, they were right. It is possible to exaggerate this change, but there was an unmistakable shift in the occupation in 1948; the new tone became more pronounced with the success of the Chinese Revolution in 1949 and the beginning of the Korean conflict the following year. SCAP now had less sympathy for the social reformers, the labor organizations, and the left-wing politicians. The purge, originally intended to eliminate prewar nationalists, was revived and directed at members of the left wing, particularly the Communists. The program of business deconcentration was abandoned and replaced by a harsher attitude toward organized labor. In July 1948 SCAP intervened to avert a general walkout by the railway and communication unions, compelling a revision of the National Public Service Law to prohibit government employees from striking.

A more important indication of the shift from reform to rehabilitation was the arrival in February 1949 of Joseph M. Dodge, a Detroit banker, brought to Japan as financial advisor to SCAP for the purpose of reviving the Japanese economy. By recommending a balanced national budget and establishment of an official exchange rate, Dodge sought to curb inflation and to

[9] George F. Kennan, *Memoirs: 1929–1950* (Boston, 1967), p. 391.

attract foreign investment. The recommendations, implemented in the summer of 1949, were strong medicine, requiring retrenchment by both government and business, and a stiffened resistance to the economic demands of labor. Owing to these measures as well as to the "red purge," which eliminated thousands of left-wing officials from government and union positions, union membership began to decline.

The most notable retreat from the idealism and the utopianism of the early occupation was the revised thinking about Japan's defense. The preamble to the new constitution had emphasized "peaceful cooperation with all nations" and had announced the intention of preserving Japan's national security by "trusting in the justice and faith of the peace-loving peoples of the world." Article 9 had codified this intention. The heady atmosphere in which these ideals were unfurled had already passed by 1948 and MacArthur had cause to regret his earlier enthusiasm. Japan, rather than China, appeared the stable hope for an alliance in Asia, and the punitive aspects of the occupation, which had largely run their course by this time, were now reversed. It no longer made sense to American policymakers to seek a weak and pacifist Japan. Therefore, shortly after the outbreak of the Korean conflict in June 1950, Japan was permitted to establish a 75,000 man paramilitary force, which was to take over from American troops responsibility for Japanese domestic security. It would not do, in light of the provisions of Article 9, to call it an "army" and so it was referred to as a National Police Reserve. Only later was it renamed the Self-Defense Force.

When World War Two ended, American policymakers commonly thought in terms of occupying Japan for at least twenty-five years in order to maintain peace and security. But the Japanese proved much more tractable to reforms than was expected, friendly relations developed, domestic pressures in the United States called for bringing the soldiers home, and MacArthur by 1947 was ready to end the occupation. Although changing perceptions of security requirements in East Asia prevented early termination, the occupation lasted less than seven years. A peace treaty was signed in San Francisco on September 8, 1951, and the occupation officially ended on April 28, 1952. Actually the de facto end had come earlier, since SCAP ceased to play a major role within Japan after the Korean conflict began in June 1950.

Though SCAP disappeared, American influence continued to dominate Japan long after the formal end of the occupation. Together with the San Francisco Treaty, the American-Japanese Security Treaty of 1952 was signed, leaving Japan in effect a military protectorate of the United States. That treaty provided for the retention of American bases and allowed Washington to use the American forces stationed there in any way that would "contribute to the maintenance of international peace and security in the Far East." It prohibited Japan from granting military bases to any other power without American consent.

This passive and dependent role was consonant with the confused and pacifist mood of postwar Japan. But it also suited its national self-interest. Adopting an essentially nonpolitical posture allowed Japan to define its national aims in narrow economic terms and thus to concentrate the energy of its people on the tasks of improving their material livelihood.

THE EMERGENCE OF POSTWAR JAPAN

13

Economic Success

The single most noteworthy fact about postwar Japan has been its extraordinary economic growth. At the end of the war, output had been reduced to pre–World War One levels. Statistics show the remarkable pace of recovery: from 1946 to 1954 real national income grew at an average of 10.8 percent, an impressive rate, but it took this achievement simply to return to prewar levels of productivity, of national income, and of personal consumption. Having regained its former level by 1954–1955, the economy then maintained an astonishing rate of growth for the next fifteen years: 9.1 percent for the 1955–1960 period, 9.8 percent for the 1960–1965 period, and 12.1 percent for the 1965–1970 period. During the two decades after 1950 the real growth rate averaged over 10 percent—nearly three times as fast as the growth of the American economy during the same period.

In the course of this remarkable expansion the structure of the economy underwent a fundamental transformation. Inevitably the relative share of agriculture, forestry, and fishing declined rapidly, while manufacturing and construction experienced a sharp rise. During the prewar period, although the importance of machinery and armaments was growing, cotton and silk textiles had continued to dominate the manufacturing sector, but by the 1960s manufacturing output was diversified and sophisticated, developing aggressively in a variety of areas, such as shipbuilding, optics, iron and steel, chemicals, machinery, and consumer durables.

What were the dynamics of rapid economic growth?

In the first place, the productivity of the economy rose rapidly, owing to extensive technological innovation. In part that was the unavoidable result of having to replace so much of Japan's industrial capacity, which had been destroyed by the wartime bombing. Since the beginning of the Pacific war, Japan had been cut off from most of its Western industrial contacts, and by the 1950s a large body of Japanese engineers and skilled technicians was ready and anxious to close the technological gap that had opened in the intervening years. As G. C. Allen writes:

Between 1950 and 1962 1,998 contracts for technical cooperation had been signed with foreign firms, nearly two-thirds of them American. Most of the contracts related to projects in industries that have grown especially fast, notably iron and steel, petrochemicals, chemical engineering, electronics, and motor manufacturing. The result was that by the early 1960s the technical gap had been virtually closed in most branches of industry and Japanese firms were themselves beginning to devise important innovations.[1]

A second driving force behind economic growth was the high rate of investment. A large share of the gross national product was plowed back into new plant and equipment facilities in order to achieve further growth. Investment was particularly heavy in export industries and capital goods industries, where demand was strong and the market favorable. A critical factor that permitted the unusual amount of investment was the high rate of saving achieved by the Japanese. In comparative terms, personal saving of Japanese during the 1960s averaged as much as 18 percent of disposable income, while Americans in the same period averaged between 7 and 8 percent. There are many reasons for this high rate of saving, including the semi-annual lump-sum bonus payments, the relatively underdeveloped consumer financing institutions, and the inadequate retirement programs. Personal and corporate saving together permitted a high rate of investment.

The third important ingredient of postwar economic growth was Japan's ample supply of highly motivated and well-educated labor. Millions of Japanese returned from overseas to swell the ranks of labor, and by the 1960s the effects of the postwar baby boom were evident in the rising proportion of young men and women in the labor force. As a consequence, wages did not rise rapidly and did not outstrip productivity. Labor moved to more productive sectors of the economy. The number of agricultural workers declined between 1950 and 1965 by 4.6 million, and over the same period the percentage of the labor force employed in small firms experienced a similar decline. Furthermore, the motivation of the labor force—the willingness to work long and hard and the strong sense of loyalty to one's firm—has caught the attention of labor economists in many other industrialized countries.

A fourth cause of added strength for the Japanese has been the overall growth of international trade. In contrast to prewar times when protectionist sentiment carried the day in many countries, the postwar reduction of trade restrictions has caused a rapid expansion of world trade. Between 1953 and 1965 Japanese exports grew an average of 17 percent a year. This impressive performance was the result of much careful and deliberate planning by both government and business to make commodities for which there was strong world demand and to achieve price competitiveness through efficient production. Accordingly,

[1] G. C. Allen, *Japan's Economic Expansion* (London, 1965), p. 109.

as we have said, Japan abandoned its former concentration on textile exports and turned instead to such new goods as transistor radios, cameras, color television sets, and automobiles.

Finally, a number of other factors promoted rapid growth. The role of government is surely one of the more important. Government encouraged growth through a wide variety of measures, including tax concessions for the corporate sector, attractive loans to leading industries, and what is called "administrative guidance" exercised by the Ministry of International Trade and Industry (MITI). In order to strengthen Japan's competitive ability in the export market, to promote technological change, and to enforce efficient use of resources, MITI encouraged mergers and various kinds of collusive arrangements among the largest firms. Another factor frequently singled out to help explain the unusual growth is the small allocation required since 1945 for national defense—less than 1 percent of the gross national product (as compared with 6 percent in the prewar days). Substantial resources were thereby freed for investment in more productive industries. Another, fortuitous factor in Japanese growth was the stimulative effect of the Korean conflict. The war created a boom in textiles, cement, and iron and steel industries. Overall, it had the effect of priming the pump and injecting much needed dollars into the economy, giving it the start on a record of sustained, rapid growth over the next two decades.

Workings of the New Political System

For all the revolutionary changes made by the occupation in the formal political institutions, party politics in the postwar period displayed remarkable continuities from prewar days. On the surface there was much turmoil and confusion; everything seemed new. In the first postwar election in April 1946 over three hundred parties participated. There were over twenty-seven hundred candidates for the lower house, over half of whom were independents or members of minor parties. Over 80 percent of the House members elected in 1946 were newcomers. The purge appeared to have wiped the slate clean to permit the emergence of a new political elite.

Ironically, however, the purge was not used extensively against the bureaucracy owing to the decision of SCAP to keep the Japanese government intact and to rule through it. As a consequence, after many of the former politicans were purged, veteran bureaucrats moved into positions of leadership in the conservative parties. Shidehara Kijurō, Yoshida Shigeru, and Ashida Hitoshi, who had served in the Foreign Ministry in prewar days and were associated with the pro–Anglo-American clique, emerged as leaders of the conservative parties. The power and influence of those members of the old bureaucratic elite were considerably enhanced by the inexperience and confusion of the Diet, which was heavily populated with freshmen. In the prewar days, the bureaucracy had been rivaled by the military and the zaibatsu, but those elites had been primary targets of the purge, leaving the bureaucrats in a dominant position. Since the turn of the century, when Itō Hirobumi left the oligarchy to form the Seiyūkai Party, it had been common for the conservative parties to draw much of their leadership from former bureaucrats. That practice was all the more common in the postwar period.

There were other elements of continuity, as well. While the number of new parties was staggering, the pattern that soon emerged showed a remarkable likeness to the prewar situation. Two conservative parties, the Liberals and the Democrats, both with prewar roots, re-emerged, and an amalgamation of prewar left-wing parties, the Socialists, also came to the fore. Although the Socialists came briefly to office in 1947, they were unable to translate the social conditions and reforms of the postwar period into an opposition party capable of holding power. Instead, they consumed their energies in ideological struggles to which a majority of the public was indifferent, at best. In contrast, the conservative parties, benefiting from the "reverse course" and the ensuing prosperity, pursued pragmatic policies that proved more in accord with the dominant impulses of the public. In 1955 the conservative parties merged to form the Liberal Democratic Party (LDP), which, for the next two decades, easily controlled a majority of the seats in the lower house.

Because the LDP has so dominated the postwar political scene, it is important to examine its intraparty decisionmaking process, for here is where the most meaningful competition and struggle has taken place. Far from being a unified party, the LDP is more like a federation of seven or eight semiautonomous factions. Loyalty to the faction and its leader outweighs loyalty to the party, for members of the faction depend on it for funds necessary to secure and hold office. The competition and relationships among the various factions decide the distribution of power and positions in the party and in the executive positions in the government. The president of the party becomes the prime minister. The latter is rarely able freely to take policy initiatives on important matters. Rather, because of the factional divisions within his party, he must build consensus on policy before undertaking new departures.

Following the "reverse course" and SCAP's decision not to pursue its policies for deconcentrating Japanese industry, there was a gradual recovery of the influence of businessmen in politics. In the prewar period, as we have seen, the great zaibatsu provided the overwhelming bulk of the financial support required by the conservative parties to carry out their activities. Since the 1950s the LDP has drawn its support from a much broader base of business interests. In most regards the business world is now a much more complex place, owing to its greater diversity, but its influence remains greater than in most other private enterprise countries. We have seen that government was heavily involved in promoting the rapid growth policies pursued by the private sector. Conversely, business leaders have been closely linked with many (though not all) aspects of the policy-making processes.

Despite the fact that since the end of the occupation the party and business elites have recovered a large measure of their prewar influence, a strong case can still be made for the bureaucratic elite as the real powerholder. One political scientist has recently written that "in Japan, despite the fact that the constitution gives this power [to make laws] exclusively to the elected members of the Diet, it is the bureaucrats who actually initiate and draft virtually all important legislation. They also contribute significantly to the passage of bills within the Diet and possess extralegislative ordinance powers that are almost on a par with the statutes themselves."[2] A former vice-minister arrogantly but with some justification characterizes the Diet as no more than an "extension of the bureaucracy." The power of the bureaucracy throughout modern Japanese history has been exercised through its penetration of the political parties. Roughly a third of the forty-odd prime ministers since the 1880s have been recruited from the ranks of high civil servants, although since the war the ratio is closer to a half than to a third. We have seen also that among all the elites the bureaucracy was the prime beneficiary of the occupation and thus entered the postwar period in an advantaged position. It has been able to maintain much of its strength despite the re-emergence of the party politicians, in part because the attention of politicians is so deeply absorbed by factional competition.

Another important area in which the bureaucrats have

[2] Chalmers Johnson, "Japan: Who Governs? An Essay on Official Bureaucracy," *Journal of Japanese Studies* (Autumn 1975), p. 10.

acquired influence since the war is through the proliferation of public corporations, which are established to supervise various aspects of the national economy—the Japan Housing Corporation, Japan Highway Public Corporation, Forest Development Corporation, New Tokyo International Airport Corporation, and so on. They number well over a hundred and are increasingly, in the view of many observers, diminishing the functions of local government, which had been expanded by occupation reforms. The corporations are, typically, planned by bureaucrats in one or another ministry; they are then staffed at the higher levels by retired bureaucrats, and controlled by the ministries.

Growth of a Meritocracy

For generations the Japanese have placed a very high value on education, partly because it was one of the main means for social advancement. But more than ever before, in the postwar period there has been an explosion of educational opportunities and aspirations. Occupation reforms lessened many of the old economic and social restrictions, reduced the inequality of income distribution, and helped create a more fluid society in which the incidence of social mobility between generations was significantly greater. Who was to advance in society came to be determined largely by academic success. Japan moved very far toward becoming a full-fledged meritocracy, that is, a society that allocates power on the basis of performance. As a result, education in preparation for the highly competitive university entrance examinations has become a major preoccupation of both parents and children. "No single event, with the possible exception of marriage, determines the course of a young man's life as much as entrance examinations, and nothing, including marriage, requires as many years of planning and hard work."[3] Education has dominated many aspects of Japanese social life because, more than any other factor, it was one's education that determined what share one was to have of the vastly increased national wealth. In the period from 1952 to 1968 the number of students attending institutions of higher learning more than tripled, and by 1974 Japan had a higher percentage of the twenty to twenty-four year old age group attending school than any other major country except the United States. The driving force behind this almost universal desire for more higher educa-

3 Ezra Vogel, *Japan's New Middle Class* (Berkeley, 1971; rev. ed.), p. 40.

tion was the rapid growth of personal income and the ambition of parents and children for social advancement.

Competition for entrance into the best universities today is extremely keen and is based on the rigid standard posed by entrance examinations, which assume special importance in Japan because a steep hierarchy of prestige is recognized among the universities. Employers with the most to offer recruit from the top universities, which are generally the old imperial universities. Those universities, being able to offer the graduates superior careers, attract the brightest students to take their entrance examinations. Owing to the ingrained pattern of lifetime commitment to one firm, it becomes critical which university one enters, for that will determine not only the kind of initial job one will have but also usually one's lifelong employment.

The pressure on students taking their university entrance examinations is therefore intense. They must try to get into a university as high up the prestige scale as possible, for not only the next four years are at stake, but their whole lives. The period of *shiken jigoku* (examination hell) each year is accompanied by all kinds of manifestations of the anxiety and psychological burden imposed on both children and parents. One of the more bizarre cases was the discovery in 1975 of a father in woman's dress taking the examination for his daughter! Those students who do not succeed often try again the following year, in the interim attending a special preparatory school. Only about two-thirds of the students succeed in their first try.

Preparation for the examinations begins very early in a child's life in the parents' efforts to gain admission to schools that are known as most successful in preparing students. As a consequence, entrance examinations are now given at every level of schooling—even in many kindergartens. If one gains admission to an elite kindergarten, presumably that will help in preparing for examination to a leading primary school and success farther up the educational ladder. An increasing number of children at every level of schooling also attend private schools (called *juku*) after regular school hours. The juku (which, for example, were attended in 1975 by over half of the sixth grade children) specifically prepare for entrance examinations at the various levels of schooling, and the success rates of the various juku are tabulated and widely discussed in the media. These cram schools have come to be a flourishing, multibillion-yen business.

How the student actually performs when he does enter the university is less important than the fact that he has arrived at one with a reputation well known by all prospective employers.

The main function of the university system in Japanese society, in other words, is not so much to educate students as to rate them according to their ability and diligence, represented by success in the highly competitive entrance examinations. Employers find in those test results a measure of a student's innate ability, his quickness to learn, and his degree of persistence in a lengthy process.

Some observers, however, feel that the examination system does not offer the equality of opportunity that most Japanese suppose it does. They point to the fact that the more well-to-do families are able to afford the tutors and juku that will enhance the chances of success in the examinations. Other observers of the meritocracy fear that it has future dangers for Japanese society, that because of the hereditary element in ability and because of the arranged marriage system, the bright will tend to intermarry with the bright and a rigid class system may develop. Dore writes that this "seems to me a danger that might well increase as the proportion of people getting to the top who were the sons of the people who got to the top increases. The danger will increase because, the more class position becomes hereditary, the greater the likelihood of sharp cultural differentiations occurring between the classes, and the greater the likelihood of antagonism resulting. In short, there seems to me a chance of Japan developing a class system with differentiations as sharp as in the class system which developed in Britain in the 19th century."[4]

However this may be, the surge of educational aspirations in the postwar period has left its mark on Japanese society. It has, for example, contributed to another noteworthy characteristic of the postwar period—the rapid decline in population growth. The immediate postwar years saw the restoration of family life and a baby boom of some proportions, but beginning in 1950 the birth rate began to drop sharply. By the mid 1950s Japan had one of the lowest birth rates in the world, and it still has. During the two decades from 1952 to 1972, the average number of children per nuclear family declined from 3.30 to 1.92. The changes wrought as a result in Japanese social life are many. One of the most important, for example, has been the change in the life of the "typical" Japanese woman. Statistical studies show that in 1940 she completed her education at the age of 14.5, married at the age of 20.8, and had almost 5 children between ages 23.2 and 35.5. In 1972 the average Japa-

[4] R. P. Dore, "The Future of Japan's Meritocracy," *Bulletin of the International House of Japan* (October 1970), p. 49.

nese woman completed her education at 18.5, married at 23.1, and had two children between ages 25.3 and 27.9. Births, in other words, are bunched so as to free the mother to work and thus contribute to the cost of educating her children.

Many reasons may be offered for the decline in the fertility rate. One group of reasons clusters around new concepts of family life. In prewar days it was a patriotic virtue to produce large families, but since the war the prevailing ethic has emphasized limiting family size. In 1948 the Diet passed the so-called Eugenics Protection Law, which aimed at disseminating information about birth control and contraceptive equipment, and which also in effect legalized abortion. The desire to improve one's standard of living became a legitimate goal, pursued with such frenzy that it was sometimes criticized in the media as "My Home-ism." People sought consumer durables—color television, refrigerators, washing machines—and better housing; and this required decisions about savings and consumption that, one way or another, affected the number of children wanted in the family. Similarly, it has become less common to depend on one's children in old age, less common to have three generations under one roof, thereby necessitating substantial savings for retirement. At the same time, the increased competition for quality education has consumed a very large part of a family's budget and, at the very least, has reinforced the propensity to limit the number of children in each family. Surveys made in recent years of the reasons for Japan's high rate of individual savings show that one of the two most important reasons influencing family saving is the desire to provide for the children's education.

Japan in the World

We have discussed a number of noteworthy themes in postwar Japan—the dynamics of its extraordinary economic growth, the dominance of the bureaucracy, the pervasive influence of education and the examination system. We may, in conclusion, turn to one final theme that is particularly striking—the confusion and uncertainty among Japanese about their ultimate mission and meaning in the world. We have seen earlier in the book that, prior to achieving a full-blown conception of national identity at the turn of the century, Japan went through a time of searching and debating various ideas of its role in the world. The postwar era has seen a search somewhat akin to that earlier time.

The content of education, for example, raises questions of Japanese identity. In reaction to discredited nationalist ideology, history was rewritten so as to no longer teach about the glorious reigns of former emperors or the exploits of the Japanese military. Supposedly, history was to be "objective," to convey a critical knowledge of the development of Japanese institutions. In fact, however, because school teachers were organized into a powerful trade union dominated by radical left-wing leaders, history texts often reflected the political bias of teachers and thus emphasized economic exploitation and "the struggle of the people" for freedom from the oppression of despotic ruling classes. For example, an historical account of the Russo-Japanese War might well avoid mention of Admiral Tōgō, the naval hero of the war, and instead concentrate on the handful of socialists and pacifists who opposed the war. The new textbooks, which have been the subject of much controversy, thus gave great play to anti-establishment figures in Japanese history —trying to find roots there for an indigenous democratic tradition. In this way, the emphasis was no longer on Japanese distinctiveness. There has been a continuing ideological struggle between the left wing and the right wing, particularly between the radical leaders of the Japan Teachers Union and the conservative officials in the Ministry of Education, as to whether "the teaching of history should concentrate on the miseries of the nation's past or on its glories, whether it should emphasize the doings of the rulers or of the ruled, whether it should inculcate the values of patriotism and dedication to national progress or of resistance to authority and the establishment of individual rights."[5]

The signs are everywhere apparent that the negative image of the nation's past and of its traditional cultural values, which has been prevalent in these textbooks, is frustrating to many Japanese. There is a belief that postwar reforms—particularly the constitution and the new education—went too far. "Postwar changes," writes a professor at Kyoto University, ". . . destroyed all the beautiful and refined customs and consciousness uniquely Japanese. . . . The cultural traditions that our nation had built through its three thousand years of history have become almost extinct. The educational system and methods that once trained our unique Japanese minds and bodies are gone. What is left is technology and a loss of nationality."[6] There is widespread self-criticism that Japan lives in a spiritual and moral vacuum, with no guiding principles other than eco-

[5] R. P. Dore, "Textbook Censorship in Japan," *Pacific Affairs*, XLIII (Winter 1970–71), p. 550.
[6] Quoted in Hiroshi Wagatsuma, "Problems of East and West in Modern Japanese Culture," unpublished paper, 1972.

nomic rationality. Ishihara Shintarō, the popular novelist who came rather close to being elected governor of Tokyo, and who was appointed to the cabinet in December 1976, plays on this theme again and again in his writings: "There is a spiritual void at the core of the Japanese nation, a moral degeneration that characterizes everything that goes on in this society."[7] Likewise, the vocal industrialist Matsushita Konosuke calls repeatedly for a redefinition of national purpose and mission: "Since the end of the war we have been preoccupied with the reconstruction and development of material aspects of our society, and have hardly reflected on our state of mind. The autonomy of a nation is based upon its traditions. In contemporary Japan the traditions have been all but ignored, and even replaced by the customs and thoughts of foreign lands. Those who grow up in present day Japan are no longer Japanese but a group of people without selves and without self-confidence. . . ."[8]

Thus, paradoxically, even as the Japanese grow more and more involved in the world through commercial contacts, through participation in international organizations, and through the ease of overseas travel for the average people, their own sense of distinctiveness, of aloofness, of being alone in the world is reasserting itself. The early 1970s was a time of particularly marked introspection. Scores of books were published concerned with questions of the so-called Nihonjin-ron—that is, what does it mean to be Japanese? who are we Japanese? where did we come from? where are we going? A number of events seemed to trigger this "introspection boom." One was the dramatic suicide of the novelist Mishima Yukio in November 1970 after he had excoriated his countrymen for their materialism, their spineless foreign policy, for their desertion of the true and pure Japanese values of the past—above all, devotion to the imperial institution. Recent archeological discoveries, including the opening in March 1972 of a hitherto uninvestigated mausoleum of a seventh-century Japanese Emperor at Takamatsuzuka in Nara Prefecture, have re-opened questions about the origins of the Japanese people, their culture, their language. Yet another contributing factor to this most recent period of self-examination was the return of two Japanese soldiers from Pacific islands, where they had been hiding out for almost thirty years. Their behavior and attitudes recalled prewar values of self-sacrifice and absolute loyalty to the Emperor—values whose loss was lamented by many Japanese.

---

[7] Ishihara Shintarō, "A Nation Without Morality," in *The Silent Power: Japan's Identity and World Role* (Tokyo, 1976), pp. 75–95.
[8] Quoted in Wagatsuma, "Problems of East and West."

The focus of much of this frustration has been Japan's low-profile foreign policies. For the whole of the postwar era, Japan has been a military protectorate of the United States. Despite the gradual build-up of its Self-Defense Force, Japan remains the weakest state in Northeast Asia—weaker than Taiwan and North and South Korea. Thus the third greatest economic power in the world has maintained a muted voice in the realm of international politics. Nor is there any strong disposition on the part of its leadership to abandon this low visibility, for bold or decisive moves in the international field would inevitably be divisive and disruptive at home.

Such an image of impotence and dependency continues to frustrate a great many Japanese. Nationalism in the postwar period has tended to take the form of anti-Americanism and neutralism, a desire to be free of United States domination. Such sentiments have periodically surfaced, most notably in 1960 when the United States-Japan Security Treaty was up for renewal. At that time massive demonstrations of opposition took place all over the country. Again, during the student demonstrations of the 1960s and 1970s, one element of protest was directed at the dependency relationship with the United States. Charles de Gaulle's disdainful reference to Prime Minister Ikeda Hayato as "a transistor salesman," or the frequently heard slight that "Japan behaves more like an international trading company than a nation state"—such remarks wound the pride of a highly sensitive people. It is difficult to predict what combination of circumstances in the international environment and in domestic politics will bring the Japanese elites to lead their country to a much more resolute nationalist posture. What seems sure is that it is only a matter of time.

SUGGESTIONS FOR FURTHER READING

General Works

There is now a very substantial literature in English on the history of modern Japan. A number of general surveys can be recommended. John Whitney Hall, *Japan: From Prehistory to Modern Times* (Delacorte, 1970), is particularly valuable for its treatment of the pre-1868 background. Two reliable accounts are W. G. Beasley, *The Modern History of Japan* (Praeger, 1973; rev. ed.), and Peter Duus, *The Rise of Modern Japan* (Houghton Mifflin, 1976). Another authoritative textbook, one written in wider setting, is J. K. Fairbank, E. O. Reischauer, and A. M. Craig, *East Asia: Tradition and Transformation* (Houghton Mifflin, 1973). Marius B. Jansen, *Japan and China: From War to Peace, 1894–1972* (Rand McNally, 1975), is a remarkable treatment of Sino-Japanese relations in the context of the modern development of the two countries. Two books by Edwin O. Reischauer are noteworthy for their readability: *Japan: Story of a Nation* (Knopf, 1970) and *The Japanese* (Harvard, 1977). A splendid book, written in 1931 and recently reissued, is G. B. Sansom, *Japan: A Short Cultural History* (Stanford, 1977). On the same subject and more current is H. Paul Varley, *Japanese Culture: A Short History* (Praeger, 1977). A standard collection of source readings is Ryusaku Tsunoda et al., *Sources of Japanese Tradition* (Columbia, 1958).

Most of the writing on modern Japan is the product of the generation of scholars writing since the 1950s and preoccupied with explaining the reasons why Japan was able to achieve rapid industrialization. An exploration of the many aspects of this process was carried on in a succession of conferences, subsequently published by the Princeton University Press as a six-volume series entitled "Studies in the Modernization of Japan." Individual volumes in the series are Marius B. Jansen (ed.), *Changing Japanese Attitudes Toward Modernization* (1965); William W. Lockwood (ed.), *The State and Economic Enterprise in Japan* (1965); R. P. Dore (ed.), *Aspects of Social Change in Modern Japan* (1967); Robert E. Ward (ed.), *Political Development in Modern Japan* (1968); D. H. Shively (ed.), *Tradition and Modernization in Japanese Culture* (1971); and James W. Morley (ed.), *Dilemmas of Growth in Prewar Japan* (1971). A critical discussion of the approach used in many of the essays in this series is offered in John W. Dower's introduction to *Origins of the Modern Japanese State: Selected Writings of E. H. Norman* (Random House, 1975). Included in the latter is Norman's classic work, *Japan's Emergence as a Modern State* (1940), which is still worth reading for the problems of interpretation it poses.

The histories of Japan and the United States have intertwined at many points in the last century. Charles E. Neu, *The Troubled Encounter: The United States and Japan* (Wiley, 1975), is the most recent of several useful accounts of this relationship.

A number of other books that treat major themes in modern Japan should be called to the reader's attention. A highly provocative essay on Japan is included in Barrington Moore, Jr., *Social Origins of Dictatorship and Democracy* (Beacon, 1966), which traces the roots of Japanese fascism to the way in which agriculture became commercialized. Ivan Morris, *The Nobility of Failure* (Holt, Rinehart, and Winston, 1975), explores the Japanese attachment to tragic heroes in history who chose defeat and death rather than compromise their ideals. Tetsuo Najita, *Japan* (Prentice-Hall, 1974) elucidates the dynamic tension in modern Japanese politics between bureaucratic expertise and idealistic protest. Albert M. Craig and Donald H. Shively (eds.), *Personality in Japanese History* (California, 1970), is also of related interest.

Several books on Japanese society and culture are of broad scope. The classic is Ruth Benedict, *The Chrysanthemum and the Sword* (Houghton Mifflin, 1946). An underrated but important work is R. P. Dore, *City Life in Japan* (California, 1958). A more recent controversial book is Chie Nakane, *Japanese Society* (California, 1970).

For the reader wishing to survey the development of Japanese literature, two books by Donald Keene are recommended: *Anthology of Japanese Literature: From the Earliest Era to the Nineteenth Century* (New York, 1956) and *Modern Japanese Literature: From 1868 to the Present Day* (New York, 1956). An absorbing study of the modern Japanese novel is Masao Miyoshi, *Accomplices of Silence* (California, 1974).

Tokugawa Government and Society

During the last twenty years a great deal of significant research on the Tokugawa Period has served to deepen our understanding of the highly complex government and the dynamic society that took shape after 1600. To grasp the historical influences that brought about the establishment of the Tokugawa Bakufu, the reader is directed to John Whitney Hall, *Government and Local Power in Japan, 500–1700* (Princeton, 1965), and to G. B. Sansom, *A History of Japan, 1334–1615* (Stanford, 1958). The critical role of foreign affairs in the bakufu's establishment is treated in C. R. Boxer, *The Christian Century in Japan* (California, 1951), and George Elison, *Deus Destroyed* (Harvard, 1973). Workings of the Tokugawa system of government are described in a number of works, including Harold Bolitho, *Treasures Among Men* (Yale, 1974); Conrad Totman, *Politics in the Tokugawa Bakufu, 1600–1853* (Harvard, 1967); Toshio Tsukahira, *Feudal Control in Tokugawa Japan* (Harvard, 1966); and Herschel Webb, *The Japanese Imperial Institution in the Tokugawa Period* (Columbia, 1968).

Studies of economic and social change in the Tokugawa Period are essential for understanding the background of industrialization. Readers' attention is called to two particularly important works: R. P. Dore, *Education in Tokugawa Japan* (California, 1965), and Thomas C. Smith, *The Agrarian Origins of Modern Japan* (Stanford, 1959). A useful collection of essays is J. W. Hall and M. B. Jansen (eds.), *Studies in the Institutional History of Early Modern Japan* (Princeton, 1968). The evolution of Tokugawa law is ably traced in Dan Fenno Henderson, *Conciliation and Japanese Law* (Washington, 1965). The economic impact of social change on the samurai class is the subject of Kozo Yamamura, *A Study of Samurai Income and Entrepreneurship* (Harvard, 1974). The importance of demographic change in the Tokugawa Period for understanding Japanese industrialization is studied in two new works: Susan B. Hanley and Kozo Yamamura, *Economic and Demographic Change in Preindustrial Japan* (Princeton, 1977), and Thomas C. Smith, *Nakahara: Family Farming and Population in a Japanese Village, 1717–1830* (Stanford, 1977).

Books particularly helpful in understanding the cultural currents of the period are Howard Hibbett, *The Floating World in Japanese Fiction* (Oxford, 1959), and two books by Donald Keene: *The Japanese Discovery of Europe* (Stanford, 1969; rev. ed.) and *World Within Walls* (Holt, Rinehart, and Winston, 1977).

The study of the role of ideas in Tokugawa history has lagged, but in the past few years interest in this field among several historians promises to correct that shortcoming. The recent publication of a collection of essays in Tokugawa intellectual history, edited by Tetsuo Najita and Irwin Scheiner, is one sign of the new interest. Another is the translation of one of the major academic works in Japan on this subject: Masao Maruyama, *Studies in the Intellectual History of Tokugawa Japan* (Princeton, 1974). Robert N. Bellah, *Tokugawa Religion* (Free Press, 1957), is a provocative study of Japan's preindustrial values. Another work is David M. Earl, *Emperor and Nation in Japan* (Washington, 1964).

The Meiji Restoration

The Restoration is surely one of the most complex and problematic events in modern history. Research in the last decades has gone a long way toward demystifying the circumstances surrounding it. The reader would do best to turn first to W. G. Beasley, *The Meiji Restoration* (Stanford, 1972), which has the virtues of synthesizing much of the voluminous research and offering an overview that carries the story through to 1873. Various aspects of the restoration are analyzed in several other excellent works. Albert M. Craig, *Chōshū in the Meiji Restoration* (Harvard, 1961), approaches the event from an analysis of one of the two leading anti-Tokugawa domains. Marius B. Jansen, *Sakamoto Ryōma and the Meiji Restoration* (Princeton, 1961), builds its account around one of the leading activists. Harry Harootunian, *Toward Restoration* (California, 1970), studies the growth of political consciousness that became an essential ingredient of the restoration movement. Finally, the reader would do well also to consult Professor Beasley's earlier work that concentrates on the role of foreign affairs in bringing on the restoration: *Select Documents on Japanese Foreign Policy, 1853–1868* (Oxford, 1955).

Japan's Cultural Revolution

The standard work for many years on the cultural impact of the West on Japan in the early Meiji Period has been George B. Sansom, *The Western World and Japan* (Knopf, 1950). More recently a number of good books have been published that provide an understanding of this period of "civilization and enlightenment." Fukuzawa of course is the central figure. The interested reader will want to consult the study of his ideas by Carmen Blacker, *The Japanese Enlightenment* (Cambridge, 1964), as well as *The Autobiography of Yukichi Fuku-zawa* (Schocken, 1972) and the translations of two of his important works: *An Encouragement of Learning* (Sophia, 1969) and *An Outline of a Theory of Civilization* (Sophia, 1973). Also useful is William R. Braisted, *Meiroku Zasshi: Journal of the Japanese Enlightenment* (Harvard, 1976). Two useful biographies for understanding the intellectual bureaucrats of this period are Thomas R. H. Havens, *Nishi Amane and Modern Japanese Thought* (Princeton, 1970), and Ivan Hall, *Mori Arinori* (Harvard, 1973). Books treating the interaction with Western culture later in the Meiji Period include Fred Notehelfer, *Kōtoku Shūsui: Portrait of a Japanese Radical* (Cambridge, 1971); Kenneth B. Pyle, *The New Generation in Meiji Japan* (Stanford, 1969); and Irwin Scheiner, *Christian Converts and Social Protest in Meiji Japan* (California, 1970). The origins of the modern novel in this period are treated in two books by Marleigh Ryan: *Japan's First Modern Novel* (Columbia, 1967) and *The Development of Realism in the Fiction of Tsubouchi Shōyō* (Washington, 1975).

Political Developments

The origins of Japanese constitutionalism have been the subject of much controversy. Three standard works are George M. Beckmann, *The Making of the Meiji Constitution* (Kansas, 1957); Nobutaka Ike, *The Beginnings of Political Democracy in Japan* (Johns Hopkins, 1950); and Robert A. Scalapino, *Democracy and the Party Movement in Prewar Japan* (California, 1953). Their interpretations have been challenged by George Akita, *Foundations of Constitutional Government in Modern Japan, 1868–1900* (Harvard, 1967). Further useful reading would include Roger F. Hackett, *Yamagata Aritomo in the Rise of Modern Japan* (Harvard, 1971); Joseph Pittau, *Political Thought in Early Meiji Japan* (Harvard, 1967); and Bernard S. Silberman, *Ministers of Modernization* (Arizona, 1964).

The rise and fall of political parties after the turn of the century can be traced in three fine books: Tetsuo Najita, *Hara Kei in the Politics of Compromise, 1905–1915* (Harvard, 1967); Peter Duus, *Party Rivalry and Political Change in Taishō Japan* (Harvard, 1968);

and Gordon M. Berger, *Parties out of Power in Japan, 1931–1941* (Princeton, 1977). Frank O. Miller, *Minobe Tatsukichi* (California, 1965), relates the thought of one of the parties' major ideologues.

Industrialization and Its Social Consequences

The standard account of the beginnings of Japanese industrialization is Thomas C. Smith, *Political Change and Industrial Development in Japan: Government Enterprise, 1868–1880* (Stanford, 1955). Also of interest is Johannes Hirschmeier, *The Origins of Entrepreneurship in Meiji Japan* (Harvard, 1964). In the text I have made reference to a number of important articles by Crawcour, Landes, Rosovsky, Patrick, and Yamamura that relate to controversies over the role of the state and private enterprise in initiating industrialization. The reader should also consult William W. Lockwood, *The Economic Development of Japan* (Princeton, 1968), as well as Lockwood (ed.), *The State and Economic Enterprise*, mentioned earlier. Byron K. Marshall, *Capitalism and Nationalism in Prewar Japan* (Stanford, 1967), and Hugh Patrick (ed.), *Japanese Industrialization and its Social Consequences* (Berkeley, 1976), are important additions to this literature.

The social history of the interwar years has only begun to receive the attention it deserves. Bernard S. Silberman and H. D. Harootunian (eds.), *Japan in Crisis* (Princeton, 1974), contains a number of valuable essays. The left-wing reaction to social problems is dealt with in a number of books: George M. Beckmann and Genji Okubo, *The Japanese Communist Party, 1922–1945* (Stanford, 1969); Gail Lee Bernstein, *Japanese Marxist: A Portrait of Kawakami Hajime* (Harvard, 1976); Henry D. Smith II, *Japan's First Student Radicals* (Harvard, 1972); and George O. Totten, *The Social Democratic Movement in Prewar Japan* (Yale, 1966). Tatsuo Arima, *Failure of Freedom* (Harvard, 1969), analyzes the attitudes of intellectuals in the interwar years. Gary D. Allinson, *Japanese Urbanism: Industry and Politics in Kariya, 1872–1972* (California, 1975), describes the social and political effects of the Toyota factory on its locality. Koji Taira, *Economic Development and the Labor Market in Japan* (Columbia, 1970), also contains useful analysis of the interwar years.

Imperialism and Militarism

Owing to the influence of World War Two, more has been written about imperialism and militarism than other aspects of modern Japanese history. For the first phase of Japanese imperialism from 1895 to 1914 one would do well to begin with Hilary Conroy, *Japan's Seizure of Korea* (Pennsylvania, 1960), and Akira Iriye, *Pacific Estrangement: Japanese and American Expansion, 1897–1911* (Harvard, 1972), which analyze the motivations of Japanese foreign policy in this period. Other useful studies include Marius B. Jansen, *The Japanese and Sun Yat-sen* (Harvard, 1954); Ian Nish, *The Anglo-Japanese Alliance* (London, 1966); and Shumpei Okamoto, *The Japanese Oligarchy and the Russo-Japanese War* (Columbia, 1970).

The reorientation of Japanese foreign policy after World War One is ably analzyed in Akira Iriye, *After Imperialism* (Harvard, 1965). Specific problems of diplomacy are treated in Roger Dingman, *Power in the Pacific: The Origins of Naval Arms Limitation, 1914–1922* (Chicago, 1976), and James W. Morley, *The Japanese Thrust into Siberia* (Columbia, 1957).

The sources of ultranationalism in the 1920s and 1930s have been the subject of several books. Perhaps one would do well to turn first to the relevant essays in Masao Maruyama, *Thought and Behaviour in Modern Japanese Politics* (Oxford, 1969), for the interpretations of a leading political scientist. Richard Mitchell, *Thought Control in Prewar Japan* (Cornell, 1976), shows how the Peace Preservation Law narrowed the range of political debate. Rural support for ultranationalism is studied in Thomas R. H. Havens, *Farm and Nation in Modern Japan* (Princeton, 1974), and Richard Smethurst, *A Social Basis for Prewar Japanese Militarism* (California, 1974). Mark Peattie, *Ishiwara Kanji* (Princeton, 1975); George M. Wilson, *Kita Ikki* (Harvard, 1969); and G. R. Storry, *The Double Patriots* (Houghton Mifflin, 1957), are studies of the ultranationalists. The young officers' uprising in 1936 is described in Ben-Ami Shillony, *Revolt in Japan* (Princeton, 1973).

David Titus, *Palace and Politics in Prewar Japan* (Columbia, 1974), is a valuable study of the imperial institution and of bureaucratic decisionmaking.

The international relations of the decade 1931–1941 has been the subject of more books than can be mentioned here. The best treatment of the Manchurian Incident is still Sadako Ogata, *Defiance in Manchuria* (California, 1964). Robert J. C. Butow, *Tōjō and the Coming of the War* (Princeton, 1961), and James B. Crowley, *Japan's Quest for Autonomy* (Princeton, 1966), offer contrasting interpretations of Japanese foreign policy. Stephen E. Pelz, *Race to Pearl Harbor* (Harvard, 1974), considers the influence of naval competition in the Pacific. The events leading to the Japanese-American conflict are the subject of many works, including Robert J. C. Butow, *The John Doe Associates* (Stanford, 1974); Dorothy Borg and Shumpei Okamoto (eds.), *Pearl Harbor as History* (Columbia, 1973); Nobutake Ike (ed.), *Japan's Decision for War* (Stanford, 1967); and Roberta Wohlstetter, *Pearl Harbor* (Stanford, 1962). The best book on the end of the war in Japan is Robert J. C. Butow, *Japan's Decision to Surrender* (Stanford, 1954). A study of the psychological reaction in Japan to the atomic bombing is Robert Jay Lifton, *Death in Life* (Random House, 1967).

The American Occupation

Considering how important the occupation was for both Japan and the United States, it has received surprisingly little attention. The best overview is still Kazuo Kawai, *Japan's American Interlude* (Chicago, 1960). A short study, Herbert Passin, *The Legacy of the Occupation–Japan* (Columbia, 1968), is useful for its concise analysis.

The conduct of the war crimes trials receives critical treatment in Richard Minear, *Victor's Justice* (Princeton, 1971). R. P. Dore, *Land Reform in Japan* (Oxford, 1959), is excellent. Aspects of the legal reforms are discussed in Chalmers Johnson, *Conspiracy at Matsukawa* (Stanford, 1972), and in Alfred Oppler, *Legal Reform in Occupied Japan* (Princeton, 1976). Kozo Yamamura, *Economic Policy in Postwar Japan* (California, 1967), analyzes the vicissitudes of economic reforms.

Japan Since 1952

It is not possible to mention here all the signficant works on Japan since the end of the occupation. In the realm of political developments, a number of books should be consulted, including Gerald P. Curtis, *Election Campaigning Japanese Style* (Columbia, 1971); Haruhiro Fukui, *Party in Power* (California, 1970); Nobutaka Ike, *Japanese Politics* (Knopf, 1972); Bradley Richardson, *The Political Culture of Japan* (California, 1974); Robert A. Scalapino and Junnosuke Masumi, *Parties and Politics in Contemporary Japan* (California, 1962); J. A. A. Stockwin, *Japan: Divided Politics in a Growth Economy* (Norton, 1975); and Nathaniel P. Thayer, *How the Conservatives Rule Japan* (Princeton, 1969). On foreign policy, see two books by Donald C. Hellmann: *Japanese Domestic Politics and Foreign Policy* (California, 1969) and *Japan and East Asia* (Praeger, 1972). In addition, the following books on various political topics are noteworthy: George R. Packard, *Protest in Tokyo: The Security Treaty Crisis of 1960* (Princeton, 1969); Robert A. Scalapino, *The Japanese Communist Movement* (California, 1966); and Kurt Steiner, *Local Government in Japan* (Stanford, 1965).

There are many commendable works on contemporary society. Along with Dore's *City Life* and Nakane's *Japanese Society,* already mentioned, one should read Ezra Vogel, *Japan's New Middle Class* (California, 1971; 2nd ed.) and George A. De Vos, *Socialization for Achievement* (California, 1973).

Among many good works on industrial relations, one would do well to begin with R. P. Dore, *British Factory–Japanese Factory* (California, 1973), and Robert E. Cole, *Japanese Blue Collar* (California, 1971). On specific topics, Thomas Rohlen, *For Harmony and Strength* (California, 1974), is a cultural anthropologist's study of a Japanese bank. James W. White, *The Sōkagakkai and Mass Society* (Stanford, 1970), analyzes a powerful religious and political movement. George De Vos and Hiroshi Wagatsuma, *Japan's Invisible Race* (California, 1966), is a study of the Japanese outcastes. Kazuko Tsurumi, *Social Change and the Individual* (Princeton, 1970), contains interesting essays on the social effects of World War Two.

Finally, on the Japanese economy since 1952 several books can be recommended, including Kazushi Ohkawa and Henry Rosovsky, *Japanese Economic Growth* (Stanford, 1973), and Hugh Patrick and Henry Rosovsky (eds.), *Asia's New Giant: How the Japanese Economy Works* (Brookings, 1976).

GLOSSARY

Bakufu—originally a term meaning military government, it came to designate the central administration of the country, headed by the shogun.

Daimyo—a lord possessing a han with an estimated productivity of at least 10,000 koku of rice.

Fudai daimyo—a hereditary daimyo; one who had pledged loyalty to the Tokugawa during their rise to power.

Genrō—the elder statesmen who acted as imperial advisors and took responsibility for designating prime ministers from the 1890s to the 1930s.

Genroku Period—strictly speaking, 1688 to 1704; sometimes more broadly used to designate the half century from 1680 to 1730, an epoch of brilliant flowering of Japanese culture.

Gōnō—the class of wealthy peasants in the Tokugawa Period.

Han—the domain of a daimyo.

Jōi—a slogan at the time of the Meiji Restoration, demanding "expulsion of the barbarian."

Kaikoku—a school of thought at the time of the Meiji Restoration favoring "opening the country" to trade with the Western world.

Koku—a measure of grain: 1 koku = 4.96 bushels.

Meiji Period—1868–1912.

Seiyūkai—Friends of Constitutional Government, a political party organized in 1900.

Shimpan daimyo—a related daimyo; member of a branch of the Tokugawa family.

Shishi—"men of spirit"; political activists in the period of the Meiji Restoration.

Shogun—generalissimo; originally a term designating the highest military office, it came to mean the head of the central administration in the Tokugawa Period.

Shogunate—the bakufu.

Taishō Period—1912–1926.

Tokugawa Period—1600–1868.

Tozama daimyo—an outer daimyo; one who had pledged loyalty to the Tokugawa only after the decisive battle of Sekigahara in 1600.

Warring States Period—1467–1568.

INDEX

Abe Masahirō, 51, 53
Agriculture: commercialization, 7, 27–30; productivity, 78, 79; in modern period, 115–18, 125–26
Aikoku-kōtō, 92
Aizawa Seishisai, 50
Alcock, Sir Rutherford, 79
Allen, G. C., 168
Alternate attendance system, 14, 23–25, 36, 42, 55, 59
American-Japanese Security Treaty of 1952, 167, 179
Anglo-Japanese Alliance, 106–107, 134, 137
Article 9, 158–59, 165
Ashida Hitoshi, 171
"Asian Monroe Doctrine," 144
Atomic bomb, 152

Bakufu, 11–18, 48–56. See also Tokugawa Shogunate
Banking, 31, 83–84, 86–87, 88
Beasley, W. G., 61
Bureaucracy: imperialism and, 109; in postwar period, 155, 172–73
Burma, 151
Bushidō, 26, 86

Cabinet, the, 97, 121, 159
California, 135
Castle towns, 4–7, 9, 25, 27
Chang Tso-lin, 140
Chiang Kai-shek, 147
Chikamatsu Monzaemon, 33
China, 6, 11, 17, 48, 50, 53, 64, 65, 75; war with 103, 104, 111, 112, 145–48; and Twenty-One Demands, 135; rising nationalism in, 139–48; revolution in, 150, 164
Chōshū, 13, 19, 55–56, 57, 89, 92, 94; alliance with Satsuma, 58–60; in Meiji Restoration, 60–62
Christianity: Jesuits, 1, 2, 14; ban lifted, 74
Class structure reformed, 80–81
Cold War, 164
Communist Manifesto, 112
Communists, Japanese, 125, 127, 140, 143, 156
Confucianism, 17–18, 26–27, 43, 50, 65, 99–100; reaction against, 68, 71, 73
Conscription, 90
Constitution: Meiji, 89, 92–97, 121–24, 128–32; of 1947, 158–60, 162
Coprosperity sphere, 147, 151
Craig, Albert, 19, 41, 43, 58, 60–61
Crawcour, E. Sydney, 28, 31, 79
Crisis of 1881, 94
Currency, 83

Daimyo: feudal, 2–7, 9; in Tokugawa system, 14, 18, 25–27; and alternate attendance, 24–25, 36; and Meiji Restoration, 54–55, 90
Declaration of Humanity, 156
Depression, 128, 139–42, 144–45
Deshima, 17
Diet, role of, 96, 121–23, 127, 129, 132, 159